CARE
PACKAGES

CARE
PACKAGES

Letters to Christopher Reeve from Strangers
and Other Friends

DANA REEVE

RANDOM HOUSE

NEW YORK

Library of Congress Cataloging-in-Publication data is available.

ISBN 0-375-50076-6

Printed in the United States of America on acid-free paper
Random House website address: www.atrandom.com

2 4 6 8 9 7 5 3

First Edition

Book design by Caroline Cunningham

For Will,
my most precious care package

It does me good to write a letter which is not a response to a demand, a gratuitous letter, so to speak, which has accumulated in me like the waters of a reservoir.

—Henry Miller, *The Books in My Life*

FOREWORD

As I write this it is almost exactly four years to the day since my injury turned my world upside-down. I had been injured in the past but was always relieved that all the bruises and fractured bones sustained over forty-two years never had any serious impact on those closest to me. Even when I contracted malaria on a location scout in Kenya in 1993, I only had to take three pills and spend one night in the hospital. For months afterwards, my spleen was enlarged and could easily rupture if I collided with someone in a soccer game or slid into home plate playing softball. I was told it would take some time for my spleen to process the red blood cells and return to its normal size. So I contacted the New York Giants football team and asked if they had any equipment available that would protect my spleen and allow me to carry on with sports as usual. Luckily Lawrence Taylor had the perfect device—a metal plate over three inches of foam that he kindly lent me until the start of the season. Problem solved.

But when I broke my neck on May 27, 1995, it was like entering a dark tunnel. I couldn't go in alone. My family and my closest friends would have to come with me. As we began to inch our way forward in the dark, suddenly there was light. It came from the thousands of letters that were sent to us from all over the world. Many were from old friends and people I had worked with in the past. But most of them came from complete strangers who felt compelled to write out of pure empathy and compassion. Every day during my stay in intensive care, Dana or one of our family would read handfuls of letters to me. And as I listened, I soon understood something new: that these letters were not from strangers, just people I had never met. For the first time I realized that all six billion of us on this tiny blue marble are essentially the same—in fact, it is not so hard to understand and see ourselves in others. We are only strangers if we choose to look away.

By compiling these letters and writing this book, Dana is sharing with you and reminding me of words that helped me start a new life. For that I am deeply grateful.

Christopher Reeve
1999

ACKNOWLEDGMENTS

My profound thanks go to Joseph Amodio, without whom this collection of letters would have remained only a "good idea" stashed away in thirty-some-odd boxes. A talented writer and editor in his own right, Joe spent almost two years acting as my personal research assistant, editor, sounding board, thesaurus, and cheerleader, juggling his own deadlines in order to help me meet mine. His love for the project along with his incredible patience and fastidiousness in rereading, recategorizing, and making notes on every letter made it possible for me to live my life and write a book at the same time. His enthusiasm, sensitivity, insights, and irreverent humor kept both our spirits buoyed throughout this process, especially when faced with the sometimes arduous task of making the final cuts. And, time and time again, with a loving but judicious red pencil, he saved me from my own writing. This book never would have become a reality without him.

I will be forever grateful to the lovely and spirited Wanda Chappell, who, with Harry Evans, embraced this project enthusiastically from the beginning and whose grace and charm are sorely missed. I hope the final product honors her memory.

My thanks to everyone at Random House who had a hand in

making this book: my editor, Lee Boudreaux, for supporting me every step of the way with her own unique blend of publishing know-how and Southern charm; president and editor in chief Ann Godoff for her steadfast belief in this project and in my ability to deliver it; associate publisher Mary Bahr for her calm and capable guidance; the copy editors for retaining the unique style of each letter; the design team for making this book look so good: Caroline Cunningham for the layout design, Jim Lambert for overseeing with a gentle touch, Richard Elman for his production work behind the scenes, and Andy Carpenter for the jacket design and redesign and redesign. . . .

Chris and I are blessed with a team of people making our life easier, helping with everything from Chris's physical care to child care to housecleaning to business arrangements. A huge thank-you to all of these dedicated and special people for affording me the freedom and time to sit worry-free on my office floor surrounded by letters for hours at a time.

Acknowledgment and many thanks must go to Chris's brother, Benjamin, for first coming up with the idea to save and categorize all the letters Chris received. This colossal job was then taken on by Chris's mother, Barbara Johnson, who, along with several volunteers who generously gave their time, established a mail room in a space provided by the Kessler Institute for Rehabilitation.

I am grateful to my agent, Dan Strone, for all his help and especially to Chantal McLaughlin, Dan's assistant, for her help with the enormous task of securing permissions to print these letters.

This book never would have come into being without the generosity of everyone who wrote to us. I am enormously grateful to all the people who granted permission to print their letters and to all the companies, schools, organizations, and individuals who helped us locate so many of our writers.

My thanks to Mitchell Stoller, Susan Howley, Megan Sandow, and the rest of the staff at the American Paralysis Association for storing boxes and boxes of letters and entering all the writers' names into a database just because I asked them to.

We will be forever indebted to the Charlottesville post office and University of Virginia Medical Center and their staffs for accommodating so graciously the sea of mail that poured in. Special thanks to Rebecca Lewis, Janice Brock, Dr. Scott Henson, and Dr. and Mrs. John Jane for their immeasurable help.

Finally, my love and gratitude go to my family: my parents, Helen and Charles Morosini, and my two sisters, Deborah and Adrienne, and their families for rushing to my side after Chris's accident and for never wavering in their loyalty and support; the three most amazing young people on this planet—my son, Will, and my stepchildren, Matthew and Alexandra—for their courage, love, humor, and general adorableness through thick and thin; Michael Manganiello, my soul brother, whose friendship is my anchor; and Chris, my husband, mentor, confidant, lover, inspiration, and champion, who helps bring purpose to my world. This book is in his honor.

INTRODUCTION

This book is a thank-you letter. A long overdue reply to all of the people who, during one of the most difficult and painful periods my family has had to endure, took time and wrote to us; faxed us; phoned or visited us; prayed for us; joined hands for us; sent us flowers, gifts, white light, religious tokens and talismans, books, tapes, drawings, funny stories and jokes that made us laugh, and tales of overcoming hardship that inspired and gave us hope. It is for the people who cried for us, cheered for us, sent positive energy our way—people who never expected anything in return other than the recovery of their friend and hero: my husband, Christopher Reeve.

This book is also a love letter. A love letter to Chris from me. And from the world. I hope that it will tell the story of one person's impact—in great and small ways—on a sweeping variety of lives.

CONTENTS

CARE
PACKAGES

1

IN THE BEGINNING

There are only two ways to live your life. One is as though nothing is a miracle. The other is as though everything is.

—Albert Einstein

On May 27, 1995, our life was, in an instant, inexplicably, unalterably changed. It was Saturday, Memorial Day weekend, at a few minutes past 3:00 when my husband, an experienced rider, fell from his horse while jumping a fairly routine fence and sustained a spinal-cord injury. Chris was paralyzed from the chest down and unable to breathe. As he was thrown from his horse, we, as a family, were thrown into a world we had only glimpsed as passersby: a world of loss and suffering, hospitals and emergencies. We left an able-bodied existence full of privilege and ease and entered into a life of disability, with all its accompanying restrictions and challenges. We went from the "haves" to the "have-nots." Or so we thought.

What we had yet to discover were all the gifts that come out of sharing hardship, the hidden pleasures behind the pain, the simple joys revealed when the more obvious treats and diversions that life has to offer are taken away. Something miraculous and wonderful happened amidst terrible tragedy, and a whole new dimension of life began to emerge.

All over the country and the world people began to respond to Chris's injury. Letters started pouring into the mailroom at the University of Virginia Medical Center, where Chris was being treated. Thousands of letters a week. Some from friends, former classmates, people we knew, but most from complete strangers—fans who wanted to let Chris know that they cared, or those who had shared a chance encounter with him at some time in their lives. Children sent drawings and letters in droves, worried about Superman and wishing him well. Many of the notes relayed stories of individuals whose lives had been changed by a similar injury or another type of great loss. The letters offered us comfort, humor, perspective, advice, strength, and the welcome reminder that we were not alone. We had dear friends and strangers alike pulling for us.

The overwhelming response to Chris's accident became a phe-nomenon in and of itself. The sheer bulk of mail was astonishing. By our third week at UVA, workers at the Charlottesville post office estimated that they had processed thirty-five thousand pieces of mail for Christopher Reeve. The letters came from all over, as varied in style and content as in point of origin. Some were flown from distant countries, their envelopes plastered with color-ful stamps, while stacks of penciled notes from local schools, tied with ribbon, were delivered by hand. There were long, flowery missives sent in elaborately decorated envelopes and simple, dime-store "Get Well" cards with "Superman, USA" the only address. Ultimately, we would receive at least one letter from each of the fifty states and from over a dozen countries. And they kept on coming.

As a family, we opened letter after letter and separated them by subject. Chris's brother Benjamin typed out a sheet that listed different categories and posted it in the room at the hospital where we received all the mail. Relatives or friends who happened to be visiting at the time could refer to this guide as they slit open envelopes to pass the time, in between visits to the Intensive Care Unit (ICU). We shared the letters with one another and spent hours reading them to Chris.

The letters provided solace and became a source of strength for me. I used them as tools to elevate my mood or fortify my spirit to face another day. I could go to the pile of letters marked "Funny" if I needed a laugh, or to the "Injuries" box to find tales of miraculous recoveries or, even better, advice from people in wheelchairs or on ventilators living happy, fulfilled lives.

Some of the letters were signed by groups of well-wishers: In each case, someone took the time to walk a card around and get everybody to sign.

There were other gestures of support as well: Hundreds of beautiful bouquets were delivered—too many to keep, so Chris had us distribute the flowers to other patients in the hospital. We received all kinds of gifts, from the religious—Saint Christopher medals, relics, rosary beads, holy water from Lourdes—to the secular—stuffed animals, posters, books, even a cassette of rousing Civil War songs. Ginger Sbledorio and Mary Crincoli of New Jersey sent a beautiful hand-made throw embroidered with the lyrics to Tom Chapin's song "This Pretty Planet" (a particular favorite of our family). Pat Jordan of Maine offered a coat, designed for her quadriplegic husband, who had since passed away. Each day, we had a new package to open: aromatherapy candles; an enormous pink pair of women's underpants; a model plane made of beer cans. Some gifts made us laugh; all of them touched us deeply.

People slipped their grocery money, weekly allowance, and loose change into envelopes and sent it to us. Shaquille O'Neal, a Superman fan, sent Chris one of his huge, size twenty-four sneakers with his signature. We hung it over Chris's bed. A boxer sent a glove to help Chris "fight the good fight." Sixty-eight "fellow pilots and fans" from the Johnson Space Center in Houston signed a photograph of a rocket launch. To this day, the framed photo hangs in Chris's office. It represents to him the ultimate act of defying the odds, and serves as an inspiring reminder to continue pushing the boundaries of accepted scientific knowledge.

When we left Virginia, after a month, to go to the Kessler Institute for Rehabilitation in New Jersey, the boxes of letters, faxes, drawings, and gifts came with us. And still, the mail kept coming. We set up an even more elaborate mail room that Chris's mother supervised with the help of many volunteers. While Chris and I spent our days with neurologists, physiatrists, pulmonologists, physical therapists—every "ist" in the book—learning about his care, others worked upstairs, sitting among the mountains of boxes, opening envelope after envelope. "Dear Christopher . . . ," "Dearest Chris . . . ," "My dear Mr. Reeve . . . ," or, simply, "Superman . . ."

There were times when I tried to explain the phenomenon to friends or colleagues, but I could tell they didn't really get it. The sheer quantity of mail, the consistent growth of it, the simple notion of it—that people really do feel the urge to reach out, to comfort, to share . . . and then act on that urge, actually do the reaching—was hard to believe. One had to see it.

It was around this time that I got the idea of putting together a book. These letters, I realized, needed to be shared.

And so I offer them up to you now. The chapter that follows is your initiation—a random smattering of letters on varying topics. You will read them just as we did in those first eerie, awesome days, not quite sure of who would write or what would be said next.

Chapter 3 starts off with letters from a select group of people—that special club of men and women living with paralysis, of which we were the newest members—then expands to include words from those who have endured other forms of hardship and prevailed.

The remaining chapters, like the categorized boxes in our makeshift mail room, each present correspondence on a single topic: letters written by children; notes focused on spiritual advice and support; news of potential cures and treatments; messages from Chris's fellow sports enthusiasts and colleagues in show business; and letters in response to Chris's diverse political efforts.

Sprinkled throughout these chapters you will find letters grouped by the simple heading "I Knew You When . . ." These letters, written by friends, acquaintances, even strangers who met him briefly, recall moments of Chris's life, from boyhood up to the present day. I hope a picture of the man, as I know and love him, will come into focus.

I so wish there were some way to illustrate accurately the process of creating this book. If there were, you would see an image of me, letters in both hands, letters on my lap, on all sides of me, literally moaning at the thought of having to choose one person's tender note over another's.

And, of course, after each letter was chosen, I needed the writer's permission to print it. Alas, some favorite letters ultimately had to be excluded from the collection because I was unable to locate the writers and felt their words were far too personal to print without permission. In some cases, after every attempt to contact a writer came up dry, rather than leave out a wonderful story or sentiment, I have included the letter but have withheld the writer's identity to protect his or her privacy. In these instances, you will see the letter signed with a single initial rather than a full name, city, and state.

It was an incredibly gratifying, yet fairly painful, task coming up with the final selection of letters to be printed in this book. Words cannot express my regret for all those who just missed making the cut. There were so many special ones from which to choose.

Please consider the letters on the following pages, then, as mere examples of the thousands of others, equally cherished, that remain in their categorized boxes. We have kept them all. Each one is a precious gift, a small and meaningful care package sent with love and received with gratitude and wonder.

2

THE WAITING ROOM

*You are going to be loved by people you've never seen
and never will see.*

—Flora Thompson, *Candleford Green*
(sent by Steve Lawson, Williamstown, MA)

We had been at the University of Virginia Medical Center in Charlottesville a little more than twenty-four hours when the first letter arrived. News of Chris's accident had just begun to trickle out
to the public, even though I had not released any details to the
press about the seriousness of his condition. I couldn't do it.
Stunned fear and a kind of survival instinct kept me quiet. I had
not yet reached all the family and friends I needed to contact. And,
frankly, I was just not ready to let the world inside. Like a mother
bird protecting her nest, I could only care for the two people who
needed me most: my husband, lying in a hospital bed motionless
and on life support; and my small son, who was wondering why.

It would take three more days before I would decide to accept
Ben Reeve's gracious offer to give a press conference on the fam-

ily's behalf. So I was genuinely surprised that second evening when a hospital administrator came into the room they had so generously provided for us and handed me a fax.

The short, typed message came from John Tesh, someone Chris had only met professionally and in passing. He wrote that he had heard about the accident and planned to dedicate his upcoming concert to Chris. How very sweet, I thought, that someone we barely knew would be thinking of Chris, let alone take the time to write a note.

It seemed, at the time, a unique and solitary gesture of kindness. I had no idea of the massive outpouring of love that was soon to follow, that this first brief and thoughtful note was but a single raindrop before an overwhelming, extraordinary deluge.

Dear Christopher,

It's 1:00 am and one of those rare nights when I can't fall asleep. I've been lying here thinking about you, and all the others—all those I watched being brought into the E.R. in New Brunswick last night while waiting for someone to tend to my son—who managed to dump a grill of hot coals onto his shoe. . . .

He's fine, but my heart aches for you and all those who didn't just get cleaned up, smeared with goo and sent home with a Tylenol. The newspapers and radio stations aren't saying anything anymore, but I sure am praying for your full recovery.

Forever and always, a loving

fan in New Jersey,

D.

Highland Park, NJ

Dear Mr. Reeve,

   We were shocked to hear of your tragic accident. We've been big fans of yours since your first Superman movie was released and never miss the chance to see one of your films. We enjoy seeing you portray other roles, but to us—you'll always be "our hero."

   The enclosed picture is of my daughter, Beth (then age 9), now 22, and me wearing my homemade t-shirt. We've got bowls of popcorn ready and a box of tissues close by. This was all routine gear when we watched any of the Superman movies.

   You are in our thoughts and prayers. Please get well real soon.

Your friends,

Bob and Beth Hoeltke

Buffalo, NY

Dear Mr. Reeve,

Our strength often increases in proportion to the obstacles imposed upon us. There is nothing in the world so much admired as a man who knows how to bear such obstacles with courage and hope. GET WELL SOON!

> With thoughts and prayers,
> Marilyn, David and Salvatore
> Testa, Mariann Testa Dolmen,
> and Marco Dolmen
> Grosse Point Woods, MI

Dear Chris,

To say that I am sorry for what happened to you, or that my family thinks of you on an almost daily basis and wishes you well, would minimize the impact your accident has had on our lives. I know that we are better people now; we are more sensitive and grateful for life's smallest pleasures; we grumble less at doing boring things like cutting the grass and making beds. We are really trying to appreciate our simple gift of mobility, viewing it not as a God-given right any longer, but as a cherished blessing we must notice and be thankful for each day.

When you had your accident, we cried often. I especially was saddened since I had watched your career take off from your early, early days as Ben on *Love of Life*. I watched with amazement how you built up your beautiful body to be Superman, and I cried— and still do—when I watch *Somewhere in Time* on an annual basis.

I have been married for twenty-seven years to a West Point graduate, retired Army colonel. We have an 18-year-old daughter and a 10-year-old son. I have been a college English instructor on and off for the last 20 years and have basically taken the last few years off, except for occasional part-time teaching, to stay home with our son, born after 16 years of marriage. He is the prize of our lives, like your young son is to you.

Jeffrey is a special child: brilliant, big, strong, the color of flaxen wheat and melted vanilla Häagen-Dazs ice cream. His hair is white; his eyes are kind, the color of blue topaz; his voice is gentle. Jeffrey cares about people on a mature adult level, few profundities escaping him; he is empathetic, never sarcastic or cold in the "mean" way of children.

After your accident, Jeff came into my room and handed me something for my "treasure shelf." You see, in my bedroom over the years I have placed little "gifts from the heart" from Jeff and others. The shelf is really just the sill of a high window where I started putting items more to save them from Jeff's impetuous little hands than to elevate them to "treasure" status; but as time has passed, its contents have become almost sacrosanct to Jeff, and to me. In Jeff's hands—a small, action figure of Superman.

"Here, Mom, take this for your treasure shelf," Jeff said. "Put it in the magic bowl and we'll pray for Christopher Reeve. We'll move Superman's legs and arms every day because he can't do it for himself right now."

Over and over Jeff has come into my room and rearranged the figure, who sits in the small clay bowl he made for me in first grade. I told him that the bowl was magic, that it contained all the love in the world, because it was a gift straight from his heart.

"We'll keep him strong," Jeff said. "I know if we help him exercise, it will help Christopher Reeve."

The first Thanksgiving after your accident we dried our wishbone, getting it ready for the great contest to see who would get their wish to come true. In the past, no matter what I did, I couldn't manage to let Jeff win. The recalcitrant bone always came out longer on my side. Jeff never complained, however, just saying that he was bound to win some day.

That Thanksgiving, Jeff carried the dried wishbone upstairs and stood in front of the treasure shelf in my room, saying that he was ready for the contest, not telling me why we had to move the site from the kitchen to my room. Jeff closed his eyes, scrunching them tightly, pursed his lips, and said, "Ready."

In a flash the snap punctuated the silence, and the bones were pulled apart. Of course, my wish was that Jeff could finally win and, secretly, I knew he had wished that, too.

I opened my eyes and I couldn't believe it. Jeff had the longer piece. He looked pensive and nodded his head up and down, in quiet acquiescence and gratitude.

"You won, honey," I said. "I wished that you would win. Is that what you wished for, too?"

"No, Mom, I wished Christopher Reeve would walk again," he said, as he put the pieces of the wishbone carefully back together and set them on the treasure shelf, next to Superman.

> With love,
> Cheryl Fardink
> Lakewood, TX

Dear Mr. Reeve,

I just wanted to let you know that in Austin, Minnesota—where Spam comes from—you've got a friend who cares.

> Your friend and fan,
> J.
> Austin, MN

Dear Mr. Reeve,

I know that you have received hundreds of letters since your accident, and that it is possible you will not even see this one. And yet, I need to write it. Like everyone who has heard the news, I am so saddened, and so worried for you. I am also angry! I don't think I am articulate enough to fully explain the reason for my anger. There can be no logic to a universe that will allow such a thing to happen to you. You are needed! You have touched so many lives with your craft, dignity and personal integrity. You must fight, Mr. Reeve! Fight against the capricious fates who have disabled you. Please don't let them win this one. They win so damn many!

I feel so helpless. I know that you are in the capable hands of the finest medical staff, surrounded by friends and loved ones. I know that if you need a drink of water, there is someone there to give it to you. There is someone there to hold your hand and keep reminding you that you are loved and valued. Someone will read to you if you ask. Someone will scratch the itch on your forehead. Someone will understand why you are frightened.

I can offer you none of these things, but please know that I would give them without question if such a thing were possible. All I can do is sit here on the other side of the continent and pray to gods I don't much care for, and beg them to be content with the harm they have done your body and to leave the rest of you, the best of you, alone. This I will do with every conscious breath.

A fan is such an insignificant, invisible thing. The relationship between an artist and a fan is by necessity one-sided. The artist gives, the fan takes. I have taken your gift for years, and not once have I made time to thank you for it. It doesn't matter whether or not you would have ever seen such a thank-you, or needed to hear it. It matters that I never took the time. I do so now. Thank you for

being who you are, for bringing beauty into my life, and for bringing balance to the often shallow and ugly industry you work for.

> Please live.
> Sincerely,
> Charlotte Bridges
> Redlands, CA

Dear Mr. Reeve:

I am a 26-year-old Native American from South Dakota. We
are a small reservation town of only 4,000 residents. You have many
Native American fans thinking of you and hoping for the best.

> Yours truly,
> Melanie Joy Benoist
> Eagle Butte, SD

Dear Mr. Reeve:

You have a special place in the hearts of the people of Metropolis, Illinois. Although you have no way of knowing it, you have
done a great deal for us.

In the early 1970s, the City of Metropolis [depicted in the DC
comic strip as the home of Clark Kent and his superhero alter ego]
adopted Superman as its son. A museum was opened and plans
were made for a major amusement park based on Superman.

Unfortunately, economic problems caused that plan to be
abandoned, after many people in Metropolis lost the money they
had invested in the project. Superman became a "dirty word" in
the same town that had adopted him.

But when your movie came out in the late '70s, there was a
rebirth of the Superman spirit in town. We began our annual
Superman Celebration, which has grown by leaps and bounds
throughout the years. Those Celebrations, the 15-foot statue of

Superman, and the publicity brought to the city have been very important for tourism, and for our pride. It was your movies that got us back on track.

We know that others have played the part earlier, and another actor now appears in the television series, but you will always be our Superman because of that rebirth of spirit brought about by your portrayal of the Man of Steel.

Since your recent accident, there has been an outpouring of concern from the people in the Metropolis area. We are sending a giant card, signed by more than 5,000 people from all over the U.S. who came to our Superman Celebration. We hope it will let you know how we feel and how we are pulling for you.

We know your return to health will not be easy, but we believe that you are the man who can succeed where others might fail.

> Sincerely,
> Clyde Wills
> Editor, *The Metropolis Planet*
> Metropolis, IL

Dear Mr. Reeve:

I write in deepest gratitude and sympathy. Let me tell you why. I am a 46-year-old father of one, an 11-year-old boy, Benjamin. When he was three, I introduced him to one of my childhood heroes—Superman—through you. I know you felt a little hemmed in by that role eventually, and I can understand it, but I'll always be grateful to you for the way you did it.

Superman was a huge influence on me. As a small boy I used to watch the George Reeves TV series faithfully, and often tied a towel around my neck as a cape. Later, from ages 11 to 13, I read all the DC comics fanatically. I truly believe that I internalized the values he stood for—truth, justice and the American way, in a phrase—largely because of the impact that the comic book character had on my imagination. I grew up to be a Pulitzer Prize–winning newspaper reporter, mild-mannered, bespectacled . . .

Ben is my only child. He loved your Superman films. We watched them together many times. Your portrayal exuded the decency and strength of character I hoped Superman would represent for him. I know it helped shape his view of life, and so far he is shaping up as everything a father could hope for. So in some small but important way, you influenced him. You helped. And Ben is but one small boy in your worldwide audience of millions. You did a great good.

Ben is pulling for you now. We pray for your full and speedy recovery. Reports of your strong spirits and early signs of returning reflexes suggest that maybe Superman rubbed off on you more than you knew.

> Sincerely,
> Robert A. Rankin
> Washington, DC

Dearest Christopher Reeve,

I'm thinking of you, pulling for you in your recovery. Will you let me know if you possibly can, please, what caused your horse to stop at that third jump? Will you and your brother please contact me if you think there is any possibility *whatsoever* that it was not an accident, but intentional, as I will do everything in my power to help you bring the people to justice? I believe the tragedy you are facing so nobly, so bravely, could be related to crimes committed by politicians and their staffs and people in Alabama, New York and elsewhere, under the "cover" of Iran-Contra.

> All my best,
> M.

JUNE 13, 1995

HELLO CHRIS:

I JUST WANTED TO LET YOU KNOW THAT THE MEN ON SAN QUENTIN'S DEATH ROW ARE PULLING FOR YOU. WE ARE PRAYING FOR YOUR FULL RECOVERY__ MANY OF US WERE & ARE DEEPLY UPSET OVER YOUR INJURIES. WE'RE NOT ALL TOUGH GUYS. WE LOVE YOU — CHRIS,

DOUG MICKEY

Dear Mr. Reeve,

I was so upset to hear of your accident that I just had to write to you. I have only written once to a celebrity—Audrey Hepburn, my idol, but with you it is different. You see, Mr. Reeve, you just have to get better and be yourself again. You are my link to my dearest husband, Walter, who died two years ago. We had a little "private story" between us about you.

Briefly, it went like this: I sometimes had very exciting dreams and I would tell him about them. His first response would always be "Was it me in your dreams?" I always said "yes," as it was true. One morning after dreaming, the usual question was asked: "Was it me?" This time I said, "No." He was so disappointed. He then asked "Who?" and I said *Christopher Reeve.*" He thought that was great—if it wasn't him, at least he was in fine company (as he admired you, too). So that was always our little joke.

Until my husband and I are together again, you are here for me—just seeing you and hearing about you makes me feel closer to my wonderful husband. My prayers are with you, and I know you will have the strength to go through what is happening now and be a "Super Man" again to me and so many others.

With warmest wishes,
Yolanda Darcy
New York, NY

Dear Christopher,

Ever since you starred in my all-time favorite film, *Somewhere in Time,* I have paid close attention to any news I heard about you. In addition to being an accomplished and talented actor, I had the impression that you were a *genuinely nice man.* So I was very disheartened to hear of your accident.

Please believe that stranger and more unbelievable things have happened than a full recovery from the injuries you have suffered. You and your family are in my thoughts and prayers every day. If it were possible, I think all of your fans would send a lovely pocket watch and the card enclosed would express a collective "Come back to me." My heartfelt best wishes during this trying and painful time.

Sue Myers
Sherwood, AR

The price of self-knowledge and calm is hardship and suffering. This produces the kind of freedom that money cannot buy, power cannot touch and fame has nothing to do with.

Yours sincerely,
Georgia A. Withers and The Staff
at The University Club
Washington, DC

Dear Mr. Reeve,

I was deeply saddened to hear of your horrible accident recently and wanted to express my concern. I know there are tons of people out there who feel as I do in admiring your grace, professionalism, integrity and terrific work.

You are different from most movie stars on several fronts. You have always seemed somehow less concerned with projecting just the right image or getting the most money you could out of every project, unlike my impression of many others in Hollywood.

Although I have not religiously attended every film or TV production of yours, I can quite honestly say I've always admired your strong, steady work. In fact, you're one of the few principled straight actors who, early on, didn't shy away from gay roles. As a gay man myself, I remember being pleasantly stunned way back in college when I saw you kiss the other male character in *Deathtrap*. I never sensed from you the need to proclaim your heterosexuality, however, unlike plenty of actors who have played such roles. Anyway, I just wanted to add my thanks to you for being such a mensch and a fine actor.

> With much appreciation, respect
> and fondness,
> Kevin T. Kuehlwein
> Philadelphia, PA

Dear Chris—

I am one of the thousands of people who have been keeping you and your family in my prayers over the last few weeks. You are in for a long, mentally and physically exhausting battle. As I tried to come up with something to say that didn't sound too trite, I thought of the words of Jimmy Valvano, the North Carolina State men's basketball coach turned commentator, which made an impression on me. What Jimmy Vee said went something like this: "If you laugh a little, cry a little and think a little each day, you've accomplished a lot."

Jimmy Vee was absolutely right. In our lives we get so focused on the BIG ISSUES that we forget to appreciate the value of thinking, feeling, caring and sharing—things that truly make us alive. During his struggle against cancer, Jimmy Vee also said, "Don't give up. Don't ever give up."

So Chris, you just keep laughing, crying, thinking and fighting, and I'll keep praying! May God bless you with healing, courage and strength in the days ahead.

> Lauree Padgett
> Haddonfield, NJ

Dear Christopher Reeve,

I felt compelled to write and let you know my prayers go out to you and your family. I also had to tell you what an impact you have had on me.

I know that you have been trying to shed the Superman image, but that was the first time I saw you on screen. I was just a kid, my parents were going through a divorce, and I was having a rough time of it. I went to see you in *Superman,* and for two hours I believed in magic and goodness. I believed a being like Superman existed and was watching over us mere mortals. I sat hypnotized and for a while I forgot my own problems.

That is the magic of what you do. It is important to have an escape and a chance to dream. I can't express enough what a difference you made in my life, as corny as that sounds. I have been a fan of yours from that moment on. I have watched all your films; you have allowed me to sit with you and be transported to different places and meet different people who in the course of my life I wouldn't have been able to meet. I can't thank you enough for the joy you brought to that 17-year-old boy, sitting alone in the dark those many years ago.

I wish you Godspeed in your
recovery.
Thank you,
John Benjamin
Burton, MI

Dear Mr. Reeve:

My name is Dr. Randy Eisel. I am a 32-year-old veterinarian and I live and practice in Florida. When I was in high school in Norman, Oklahoma, my friends and I were typical American teenagers. We were all (but one) from single-parent or step-parent homes, we got bored easily, had little parental restriction on our activities and thought ourselves quite clever. Individually, these character traits are not dangerous, though I recall a number of acquaintances with similar personalities who directed their energies into drugs, alcohol, truancy and other self-destructive efforts. We didn't, for one very simple reason.

Starting in 1979, five of my very closest friends—Gane Diers, Chuck Knapp, Bobby Irwin, Keeth Kipp, Carey Krause—and I all started working at the Hollywood Theater in Norman. It was, in its glory day, the kind of theater where movies were truly meant to be shown. Huge auditorium, enormous single screen, flashing marquee out front, circular drive to pick up your date, spacious windowed lobby. This theater became our "hang-out" and promoting the films our creative outlet.

For the opening of *Superman II* we decided to go all-out. We had people in costume, a "guess the weight of the Kryptonite rock" contest (actually a huge piece of lava from the front yard, spray-painted lime green), and we stitched an enormous Superman "S" to the curtain over the screen. I have probably seen that movie one hundred times. We knew all the lines by heart and would sit in the screening room and recite them along with the movie. It may sound boring, but all along we talked about the future. What did we want to do with our lives? That theater was the perfect place to sit and ask those questions. We all credit that time, that job and those movies with our staying grounded and focused.

With that in mind, I am writing to tell you how upset I was to hear about your injury. My thoughts and prayers are with you for your continued healing. As I am sure you have already found out, you have an enormous number of fans whose lives have been touched by your work, and we all want to see you back on the horses you love.

Good luck, sir,
Randy Eisel
Naples, FL

P.S.: The Hollywood is now closed and is up for sale, unable to compete with several multiplexes that came to town. Her end was not pretty but in her size and clean lines she is still regal. And there are six men—a physician, a computer-graphics artist, a recycling coordinator, an attorney, a telecommunications technician and a veterinarian/poet—who think of her—and you—often.

Dear Mr. Reeve,

I just called information for the zip code to Charlottesville Hospital and the operator immediately laughed and said, "Is this for Chris Reeve?" They are getting so many calls.

It must be so wonderful to know how many people are caring about and praying for you. We will get you well, that is a promise.

God Bless You,
Felicia Woodville
Redondo Beach, CA

I Knew You When . . .
(1961 to 1970)

Dear Chris,

I'm so sorry to hear of your accident. I want to wish you a speedy, full recovery. You *can* do it! You learned way back in third grade.

Your "old" third grade teacher
from Nassau St. School,
Gerrie (Meyer) Penrose
Mercerville, NJ

Dear Chris,

This is the umpteenth letter I have started to you. I just can't seem to get it right. I just keep thinking of you and your family at your side. You are a constant in my memories.

A snow day doesn't go by that I don't remember all the chocolate chip cookies we made in my Mom's kitchen. You would play some ditty on the piano while they were baking—something Pop Dielhenn taught you. Ta ta te te.

When my older son plays baseball, I recall the thousands of games in your backyard. Weren't you the one who hit the ball through the window of the garage behind your yard? I live now in a new development and there is no olly-olly-in-free landscaping. That was great stuff. Do kids play it now?

Remember how we walked in the snow at night—I have a photo of you then, all bright red flash-camera eyes—or those summer evenings we spent sitting on the mailbox, or the bubble-gum chewing contests on Pam's front lawn? We used to laugh all the time, and told the stupidest jokes. My sister Deborah (remember you named her "Dead-bird"?) read in the newspaper this morning that you still have your sense of humor. I would expect nothing less. So tell me—what's the joke for which the punchline was "halo statue"? That's been bothering me for years.

Every time I see fireworks I am reminded of one fourth of July. Dad let us set off firecrackers on the terrace. You were barefoot and almost stepped back onto one that you thought you had tossed forward. Didn't we put tennis ball cans over them on the driveway and try to make rockets? We were so invincible then.

We had such a great childhood. I drive down the road and get weepy thinking of what is happening to you now, and I send up a javelin prayer that you can feel God's presence and find His peace in this.

Love,
Louisa B. Huntington
Hopewell Township, NJ

Dear Chris,

I listened to your bride speak on TV yesterday and was especially moved when she said you were sitting up and watching hockey. It took me back to those great days of the Princeton Pee Wee program. John Bernard and I couldn't have been successful if it hadn't been for young boys like you, Kevin Kennedy and Tom O'Connor—eager and willing enough to be goal keepers (a very special breed)—and a host of other players.

You were a fine hockey player and you are an inspiration in your adult life—a fine actor, a great citizen and an all-round good guy.

Get well soon,
Fred Wandelt, Jr.
Princeton, NJ

Dear Chris,

Looking back at myself as an 11-year-old member of the Cleveland Lane "gang," various scattered images come to mind. You may recall that I dressed your younger brothers in tights long before you even thought of wearing them. You and Ben were already out in the world (high school) and were not part of our backyard production, *Robin Hood.* I do remember one comment you made (being a lead in high school plays, you were already the expert theater critic) after our one and only performance: "I think you need more rehearsals." The fact that no one knew their lines and my mom stood behind the large oak tree that served as backstage and whispered everyone's lines to them may have had something to do with it.

I also remember *The Music Man* at the McCarter Theater—I think you were in the train scene—and your performance in *The Boy Friend* at Princeton Day School (PDS). We knew then that you had "it." The next day, I asked for your autograph. You were so thrilled that you gave me five, each on a different piece of paper.

The fact that I can say I once lived next door to Superman is a delight. But it is the simple, spontaneous moments of my childhood, full of make-believe games and magic, that I am truly grateful for. And you and your family were a part of that.

Sincerely,
Jessica Krause
New York, NY

Dear Mrs. Reeve,

I was thumbing through some old copies of the PDS yearbook [that I inherited] following the death of Anne Shepherd, Chris's teacher. In the 1970 edition on the page bearing his senior-year image, there is a charming note, from Chris to Anne, that says a great deal about Chris himself. I have attached the text of what he wrote.

Sincerely,
Wesley McCaughan
Princeton Day School
Princeton, NJ

Dear Mrs. Shepherd: Besides being a great teacher, you have been a real friend this year and in the past—so much so that I think nothing of a "generation gap." If two people share interests and experiences, nothing else matters.

You have always placed great confidence in me. I hope I am equal to it; and I hope I never let ego get the better of me.

—Chris

3

OVERCOMING
ADVERSITY

The marvelous richness of human experience would
lose something of rewarding joy if there
were not limitations to overcome.
The hilltop hour would not be half so wonderful if there
were no dark valleys to traverse.

—Helen Keller

It was a particularly grim day in Charlottesville. The wet, gray weather outside reflected all our moods. Chris's second MRI had come in and Dr. Jane, usually sunny and optimistic, had the deflated look of a loyal and ardent fan whose team has just lost the final championship by "this much."

"This much," Dr. Jane said, pinching together his forefinger and thumb, leaving a tiny, almost invisible sliver of daylight between them. That was how much of Chris's spinal cord had been damaged. A minuscule lesion of twenty millimeters was causing all this trouble. As tiny as this lesion was, however, it was still larger than what Dr. Jane had hoped to find once the cord's swelling had dissipated. It was official now: We were in for the long haul.

———

Somehow I think I'd known that from the beginning—despite the many letters that were coming in proclaiming, "Don't believe everything your doctors tell you," and "Miracles do happen." Granted, letter after amazing letter offered miraculous tales of recovery: Debbie, from Florida, had broken her C1 and C2 vertebrae along with several other bones in her body when the DC-10 airplane in which she was traveling crashed. As is the case with most injuries that high in the spinal column, she was put onto a ventilator and given little hope that her completely paralyzed body would have any return of function.

I phoned Debbie upon receiving her fax and my heart leapt up when, after the person who answered the phone shouted, "Debbie—come to the phone! Quick! It's Superman's wife!" I heard distinctly the sound of Debbie's *running footsteps* before she picked up the receiver with her own hands, breathless from her sprint, but *breathing. Unassisted.* Maybe there was hope after all.

These stories of "beating the odds" served a certain purpose. There were dark days in the ICU when we needed to cling to the possibility that Chris's paralysis really was just a temporary state, a horrid nightmare. Surely, we would soon awaken and recall all this with a shudder, from a safe distance, spooked by our brush with tragedy and giddy with relief that it was only a dream.

But this was no dream. Today I didn't want to hear about people who were walking—the lucky ones who'd had their miracle. What we needed to do was begin to accept what had happened as a reality and create the best possible life out of these new circumstances. But how?

———

I made sure Chris was sleeping before I left his room, asked my mom to take Will—freshly napped and full of a three-year-old's manic rainy-day energy—for a swim at the Omni Hotel's indoor pool, and reached for a box full of letters, dragging it by the flaps along the gray carpet toward an armchair. Across the side of the box in red Magic Marker Chris's brother Ben had scrawled "Injuries," followed by a slash and then, underlined twice: "Inspiration."

Dear Mr. Reeve:

When I first heard of your accident a part of me felt sad that a superstar like yourself could succumb to such a devastating injury—and another part of me said, "Well, at least it didn't happen to me," and I went on with my life and thought nothing else of it. You see, I had just graduated from Penn State in May and was ready to start my life and achieve the dreams I'd had since childhood.

But a few weeks later in June, at a graduation/birthday party, my friends and I were in a lake cooling off and enjoying the summer sun when the most unthinkable thing happened. I dove off a rock into the water and landed head first into another rock. I didn't know what had happened at first, and all I could think of was, "God, please don't let me die like this." Then a hand pulled me up out of the water and rolled me over. I looked into the sky and everything hit me all at once. My God, I can't feel my legs or arms—and there was extreme pain in my neck.

I broke my neck at the C6 [cervical vertebra] level and am motionless from the chest down. [I suspect] I'm encountering some of the same problems that you are facing. We must deal with them and overcome them. I've found that friendship and the love of others is what we really need. And if a cure for this is out there we must push forward and work hard until that day comes.

I have been keeping up with your progress and pray that you continue to improve, as I do. In a way I'm glad that this has happened, because it has brought me closer to some things that I might have lost. I hope someday that maybe we can meet. Just like you, I will be walking within the next ten years, or sooner.

I'm 22 years old, grew up watching you on the silver screen, and always saw you as a childhood idol. I now see you as a real-life idol and I hope I can feed off your aggressiveness to defeat this. Your crusade against insurance companies is appreciated. Don't give up. I wish you well

Sincerely,
Steven C. Jurasits III
Saylorsburg, PA

Dear Mr. Reeve:

Six years ago the last thing I used my legs for was to hit my brakes. From that night my life changed so much I didn't think I could do it. I received letters like this in the hospital and hated the people who tried to tell me that everything was going to be okay.

I was in the prime of life—29 years old—I owned two restaurants, had the best cars, a big house and all the toys.

And in a split-second all that was useless. I went to therapy every day for a year and swore I would beat this. But every injury is different and mine didn't turn out to be a success story. I cried and cried till one day I couldn't cry anymore, and I started to live with it. It's not easy. I still have some bad days, but I found out one thing that most people don't know—I found how to be a whole person. Cars and money were not important anymore. Just being a good person, and taking each day the best I could, made me happy.

I have become an inspiration for so many people who can run and jump, and I am writing this letter to let you know that it's guys like you and me who have to keep our chins up, to help not only those with disabilities but—even more so—people who are not disabled, so they realize just how good they have it.

There is a happy ending to my story. I now own five restaurants, my two kids have their father with them and I take time to let them know how much I love them instead of running around like a crazy man all day. Life for me and my wife has gotten more special than ever. I know God will make sense of all this in your mind one day. Until then, work hard at therapy and be strong. It will get better.

> Your friend,
> Mark Khayat
> Wadsworth, IL

Dear Superman,

I have a halo on just like you do. I am 8. I hope you feel better. I broke my neck wen I was jumping on my bed. I heard about how you broke your neck, too. I am a big fan of yours.

> Please write to me when you can.
> Your friend,
> T.

Dear Christopher:

   We are writing on behalf of our son, Don, who is now a quadriplegic following a freak auto accident in 1993. His spinal cord was
severed at C4–5.

   Don was born deaf, the youngest of four children. He was an
excellent athlete, especially in hockey. The accident has taken
away his only way of communicating—by using sign language—
as he no longer has the use of his hands. He has had to take speech
therapy so he can communicate better in a hearing world. He still
undergoes physiotherapy to keep his upper body strong.

   We first heard about your accident when visiting Don in Calgary. It left us all in disbelief. We have followed your story for months ever since. We want you to know we understand the ups and downs that you and your family are undergoing. It is an uphill battle. Don is now 28 and lives in a group home. He has some very long, lonely days. But he is very independent and is currently learning how to operate his computer. He enjoys it very much. We trust this letter finds you and your family coping during this difficult time.

Yours sincerely,
Ray and Ruth Vetter
North Battleford, Saskatchewan,
Canada

Dear Christopher and family,

I spent almost the first eight years of my life visiting my dad at the Kessler Institute. He was a paraplegic—injured in a construction accident at the age of 26.

I am now 41, and wanted you to know that he and I spent the most wonderful, loving moments there in rehab. We shared his victories—which became my victories as well—and his disappointments. I made the most wonderful friends with other patients, who became my family. We were all embraced in an environment of love and support.

It is true that my childhood was not the usual, or run-of-the-mill, for sure. But it was unique, and I have always been compassionate, patient and giving because of that. (My children may argue with me on this point!)

This is probably the most difficult time you have ever encountered, but *together* you will work it out. It is the loving and sharing that matters. I learned about courage, perseverance and love from my dad and all of the wonderful people at Kessler. If I can pass on

even one quarter of that to my children, I will be so fortunate—
and so will they.

I pray that every day you all grow stronger. It has been a privilege to write this to you.

Love,
Lorraine Potente
Palisade Park, NJ

Dear Christopher and Dana,

It was with great sadness that Matt and I heard about Christopher's accident. Every time we hear of such a tragedy, we feel an immediate kinship and would like to help in any way we can. We know you have probably heard so much from all the professionals about what to expect. [But realize that] they sometimes have to be very conservative in projecting what might happen in the future.

Matt broke his neck in 1991 while playing rugby. The break was at the C3–4 vertebrae, crushing the spinal cord, not severing it, and leaving him paralyzed from his shoulders down.

While Matt is still paralyzed, he has far surpassed doctors' expectations. After a six-month hospital stay, he came home and was weaned off the respirator (now only dependent on it at night). The trachea tube was taken out and he is on nasal ventilation. Matt went back to teaching physical education (grades K–6) and coaching wrestling; he rides around in a motorized chair on the field and in the gym. At home, he uses a voice-activated computer for lesson plans and correspondence. And he keeps up with attending as many of our four girls' competitions, games and programs as possible. All this from a man who was told he might never function again.

This all came about very slowly. From the beginning of the injury I kept a journal. It was a good way to release some of my frustration and helplessness. Sometimes, when we're experiencing a difficult time I refer back to see how far we've come.

Continue to remain positive, talk in terms of recovery, and don't be afraid to ask questions of your doctors, nurses, therapists, aides or whoever is working with Christopher. Make sure Christopher realizes he is in control of his care—and life. Sometimes you may have to get a little respectfully vocal to make sure the people working with him in the trenches know he is the boss.

Never give up hope. That doesn't mean we can't get angry and justifiably question life. [But rather than] focusing on the present, we have to look to the future and concentrate on moving forward. If you ever need to talk, I'm a good listener. Our prayers are with you all.

> Sincerely,
> Peggy Moore
> Putnam Valley, NY

Dear Christopher Reeve:

You will get tired of people telling you how they know someone who broke their neck and are now normal. I won't do that. I will tell you some pearls of wisdom I have learned in the last 18 months as a quad:

1) Pick someone to tell how scared you are. Choose a person who will listen without reassuring you or saying "everything will be okay." You don't need reassurance, but you need to talk.

2) This is the one time in your life that you must be selfish. Your other life is gone for now—let the people who love you take care of it.

3) Doctors will tell you what's *not* possible. Ask the physical therapists. They don't know for sure, but we can't help asking.

4) Find the best therapy center you can. I live in New Orleans

but went to St. Joseph's in Phoenix. My 5-month-old son stayed with my sister and my husband flew in every weekend.

5) When you get depressed and suicide enters your mind, it means your body is working on getting better. Every time after feeling this type of despair, I have discovered that something new has begun to work. So go for it! Cry. Scream. It will be better soon.

The test is not the accident, but how you deal with it.

Anne Chase
New Orleans, LA

Dear Mr. Reeve,

I am 16 years old and was born with spina bifida. My parents were told that due to my serious birth defects I would never stand, sit or walk. Well, I proved them wrong about some of that.

I use a wheelchair for mobility but I also enjoy archery and have spent two years on J.V. High School Cheering. My team won first place in the Eastern States competition. It was scary being the only disabled competitor in a college gym.

Therapy can be a pain, but keep working at it. Exercise can make the most of what you have.

> With concern,
> Beth Kelley
> Hackettstown, NJ

Dear Christopher and family:

Ever since we heard of your accident, my husband and I have felt deep concern and hoped for the best. We wanted to tell you that everyone we talk to—family, friends, colleagues, neighbors—are thinking of you, too.

I feel especially deeply for you because I've been suffering on the sidelines for months with a back problem. It is minor compared to your injury, yet it has forced me to face and make peace with a measure of life's dark side. Doing this—making peace—is an enormous challenge but there are rewards in it. I learned to live in the moment and find deeper pleasure than I knew before when I was too active, too scheduled. I learned that joy is always possible, and I saw all the ways in which I was blessed despite the pain. I made peace with episodes in my life that I have regretted for years, and now feel more whole and content. Each piece of this brightness was hard-won and, therefore, rare and excellent. Beautiful.

I will be thinking of you as months go by and hoping you will regain movement but, above all, find a way to live with the situation as it evolves. Just know that so very many people care deeply. Knowing that helped lift my spirits many times.

With affection and hope—

Linda and Al Borcover

Evanston, IL

Dear Mr. Reeve,

I have never written a letter like this before, because until now I never had a reason. Today, I find myself praying for you and your family, and remembering a time when you made a difference in my life.

The rosary I have enclosed was given to me when I was in the hospital recovering from a car accident. I had just turned 12 and the doctors were not sure if I would ever walk again. The drunk driver who hit me caused severe damage to the right side of my body, as well as my skull. I was very scared and alone.

That was when you walked into my life— or, I should say, flew. My parents brought in a VCR and two of your Superman movies. They knew I liked Wonder Woman, so they decided to give it a try. I can't really say just how many times I watched those movies but, each time, they gave me something—someone to believe in. I knew I didn't have to be afraid anymore because, as long as you were a click away, I was never alone.

Today I am a college student who enjoys hiking and tennis, and believes in miracles. I have followed your career for the last 10 years and have grown to admire all your work, onscreen and off. The hero I found in Superman then is still the strong, kind person I believe in today. Healing takes a great deal of time, and it's during that process that we discover we are much stronger than we ever imagined.

I just want you to know that you do make a difference! And you will always have a friend in Grand Island. I will keep praying for you.

Very truly yours,
Susan A. Szczublewski
Grand Island, NY

Dear Christopher,

I am writing because, since your accident, you are much in my thoughts. You see, I was diagnosed with multiple sclerosis at about the same time you had your fall, and although our conditions seem dissimilar, the effects they have had on our lives are much the same.

I wish I could put my arms around you and say, "It's okay, I know." For I do know how it feels to have your life suddenly in ashes, to face all the things you can never do again. I cannot work at the job I love. I cannot run or dance or do all the things I have so taken for granted. This disease is eating away at my body. There are days I can't see, days I can't hear, feel, taste or smell.

But there are days when I can see and I watch the sun dance on the leaves of our maple tree and shine golden in the hair of my children. On the days I can hear I awaken early and listen to the birds sing "welcome" to the new day.

On the days I can feel, I lift myself to feel the breeze as it kisses my face and tickles my neck. Even when I cannot feel my husband's touch I know he can feel mine. This is what makes life precious.

The only constant I possess is my love for others. You may ask what good is that if you cannot show it? But you can. In your eyes. Even when my body won't work, when my face can neither laugh nor cry, my eyes can still shine. My heart can still overflow.

You still have your mind, your ears, your eyes, your mouth. You can still smell the flowers. You can still be. You can still do.

My thoughts and prayers are

with you,

M.

Chris Reeve:

I may have some experience that will be of value to you. I am one of the longest-term survivors of cervical spinal fusion in the U.S.

In 1952, at the age of 14, I took a rifle slug through the jaw and into my spinal column. The slug broke my jaw and damaged my spinal cord extensively. The entire left side of my body was paralyzed (as if I were split in two).

I underwent a fusion of the first and third cervical vertebrae at the Mayo Clinic. The fusion fixed the broken neck problem—but I was told that the spinal cord damage was permanent—that the cord does not regenerate and that I would be paralyzed—permanently.

Horsepucky!

I am now CEO of a corporation in California. The only effect I show of the "event" is an inconvenient stiff neck. I do everything that I want to do, including riding roller coasters and motorcycles, and enjoying gold mining, hunting, fishing, traveling and more hazardous things than most people would consider. Neither my accomplishments or desires have been impeded.

You see, Chris, I found out that the spinal cord does regenerate. It just doesn't do it in a way that the medical community understands. [It's like] the bumble bee—scientists long held that a bumble bee should not possibly be able to fly because its body mass is far too great for its wing area. Somebody forgot to tell the goddamned bee—and he has *always* flown just fine.

Remember one thing, Chris. When Eddie Rickenbacker lay near death in a hospital in Hawaii after ditching his aircraft at sea during W.W.II, he heard on a radio by his bed that he was "all through" and would not live till morning. It pissed him off so badly that he threw the radio across the room. I felt the same way and, in fact, popped out of a 15-day coma and screamed at a minister when he read the 23rd Psalm over me. *You* tell the doctors when you are through. Don't let *anyone* else tell you!!

Sincerely,
Robert D. (Bob) Zachte
Fresno, CA

Dear Christopher,

I was devastated to hear on the news of your terrible riding accident. I just had to write you to tell you my feelings about it. It will make me feel better and it might cheer you up a bit.

My son was born brain damaged. When he was young, two events affected his life. When his sister was born, he uttered his first word ("baby"). The other event was when he watched his first Superman film starring you. My son had watched TV and films before but seemed unable to take in the images on the screen. Yet he sat engrossed through your film, loved your coloured outfit and, afterward, started asking questions about planets and the world. He even started reading books. I think at that point in his life he realised that there was a living world outside his own. We collected the films and have watched them many times over the years.

Today, my son lives independently, in his own flat in a sheltered housing complex, and has a job. This is why I think of you as a friend as well as a film star, as you have been in my home (on the tele) so often.

Christopher, you *will* feel better. Try to think positive thoughts, but do not worry if you have a bad day. Everyone is entitled to a bad day. They pass.

Remember, you still have a mind of your own, with views and opinions on bringing up the children and running your life. Make *your* views known to everyone.

And, lastly, don't try to put on a brave face all the time. You have so many loving people around you wishing to help and support you through the bad patches. Just tell them how you feel.

Best wishes,

From a long-standing English fan

Dear Mr. Reeve,

I was buried in the coal mines when I was 31. When they first got me out the doctors said I might be paralyzed from the waist down. L1 and L2 [lumbar vertebrae] were broken—they fused them together with bone from my hip. It worked, though my right arm and hand didn't get better.

As bad as I was—and I didn't list all the injuries, there wasn't hardly any places that was missed—there was still people in the hospital wing that was in worst shape. The 17-year-old girl in the bed next to me will never walk again and the guy down the hall lost both legs—both were in car wrecks.

I really liked working in the coal mines because I was doing something that only a few years before women couldn't do. The law wouldn't let them. I had to work so hard to be accepted by the men I worked with. I'm only 5′5″ and 114 pounds when I was hurt. I had to work my butt off to make it happen. Then in the blink of an eye it was over.

My life was changed, but everything is not bad. My personal life is better now. I met my husband a year after and he's a great guy. I thought my life was over but it wasn't. Even if I never use my hand again, and it hurts, I'm now glad I didn't die like I wanted to at first.

I hope it works out for you. I didn't have anyone to talk to when it happened to me. Just people that had never been there. They mean well but they haven't lived it. If I can help you, call me at anytime. My friends call me Robin. I'll keep good thoughts for you.

> Lynda P. Talbott
> Elkins, WV

Dear Superman,

I'm 13 years old and hope that you never give up. Miracles do happen. I've got proof.

Somewhere in India, about 10 years ago, a little boy lived in a small village. In this village, they had almost no contact with the outside world. No electricity, medicine, etc. One day, the little boy, named Haripal, got the measles. He was only about 4. Not having had vaccinations, the condition only worsened. His parents believed he was possessed by demons. Haripal's father took him, telling his mother that he would go find help. Instead, he threw his son down a dry well.

Four days later, a pair of Mother Teresa's nuns walked by and heard a wimpering from the well. They thought it was a puppy—to their surprise, it was a little boy!

He was put into an orphanage and there he lay, on his back in a bed, for four years. At that time, Mother Teresa was passing through. Out of all the children, she spotted Haripal. She flew him out to San Francisco where he had metal rods put in his legs, so he could be placed in a sitting position.

Mother Teresa then called a friend to come and talk to him, under no obligation. (You must understand, this woman and her husband already had nine children, at least five of whom were adopted.) Nevertheless, Haripal soon became the newest addition to the household. The doctors told his new parents that Haripal would never be able to operate his own wheelchair, let alone be able to talk. (He had been rendered triplegic from the measles, having only the use of his right arm. He had also suffered brain damage as a result of hitting his head on the bottom of the well.) Despite this, Haripal's parents enrolled him in a program that put disabled students in regular schools, rather than shutting them away from view.

That's when I met Haripal. He was in my class the year before last. Within that first year, a group of us worked with him. I am now happy to say that not only does he drive his own wheelchair, he talks. If that's not a miracle, then I don't know what is.

Miracles happen. Never give up hope, Mr. Reeve. Never.

> God bless you, sir,
> Nikki Biggers
> Healdsburg, CA

Dear Christopher Reeve:

The following letter was dictated by a 37-year-old man who is a great fan of Christopher Reeve. He is active in sports and a medal-

winning athlete in the Connecticut Special Olympics
Games. He requested that this silver medal, which
he recently won in competition, be sent to
Mr. Reeve. Joe sends his prayers, courage
and warm thoughts for a speedy recovery:

> *I won the race for you. This medal is sent to you, and I've*
> *done it, a hell of a job. Next year I'll win the gold. I was running on*
> *Thursday on the road with the torch, and with the police for the*
> *Special Olympics for you. I stood up there with the torch in*
> *my big hands, raised it up over my head, and said this big*
> *race is for you, big dude. Next year I'll do it again. I did a*
> *hell of a job, my fire power did it for you. I'm sending to you*
> *my picture.*
>
> *Fondly,*
> *Joe Cuzzocreo*
> *Orange, CT*

Dear Chris,

I have a story to tell you. I was in a pretty severe head-on colli-
sion back in 1991. I downplayed it then because the only way I
could deal with the aftermath was by avoidance. I didn't suffer
much permanent damage—I dealt with memory loss for some
months, a cracked head and ribs, broken ear, smushed knee, stuff
like that. The emotional damage was tougher—I realized things
could happen to me that were not within my control.

But I gained so much. I found out who my friends really are:
They were there to take care of my son during my physical therapy, they took him skiing when I couldn't, bought my groceries,
and held me when I couldn't take it anymore. The hardest part was
thinking about what would have happened if I hadn't taken those

two seconds to fasten my seatbelt. I'd look at my son and start crying, thinking about what that would have done to him.

Every day now I tell him I love him. I show him I love him. And I let my friends know how much they mean to me. Chris, you've got the support of the entire country behind you. We all care about a man who has brought something of value into our lives. You've earned that support. Hang in there.

Bonnie Norman
Boulder, CO

Dear Christopher:

I had to write to you and share. In 1983, after four surgeries at Sloan-Kettering, the specialists decided to amputate my husband's left leg, hip and pelvis to stop bone cancer. He, like you, was a very physical person, at the height of his career at AT&T, and was devastated.

His first thoughts were of me, how he'd ruined my life, would be a burden, wasn't a man, etc.—all that B.S. you guys are taught to believe. I listened, assured him it wasn't his left leg that attracted me, and gave him five minutes to feel sorry for himself. Then we got to work.

Sloan had advised us he should accept life in a wheelchair as he'd never be able to handle a prosthesis. I'm glad they told us that—we accepted the challenge. That's when I found the Kessler Institute. I loved their philosophy: They don't take "give-ups," just those who are determined to improve (and work their buns off). I can't say enough about Kessler or their staff.

He entered Kessler barely healed, and went through physical therapy day and night to determine if he could handle a specially made prosthesis. I knew he could do it, and he did! He walked out of there and everyone cheered.

Soon, he learned to control "Lefty," as we called the prosthesis. He returned to work, but found he was no longer satisfied in the corporate world—he had other things to do. So he retired early and went into amputee services as a volunteer. He felt he was on borrowed time and had to give back for the life he almost lost.

I can't begin to tell you all the things he accomplished. He became an amputee counselor and was so happy and fulfilled, meeting exceptional, inspirational people we would never have known in our other lives.

Our lives did change. Little details no longer were important. We lived each day to the hilt. We loved more deeply, we joked, we laughed, we accomplished things together. We were together every day, 24 hours, and we loved every bit of it. Those 11 years on "borrowed time" were a beautiful gift.

I lost him last year. The cancer returned and in a month's time he left us. But what he left was a legacy of courage, determination, unselfishness—the strength of the human spirit. I miss him, but I do not grieve. We were so lucky. We were given a second chance and made the most of it.

Now you and your wife are in similar circumstances. I am so sorry this had to happen to you, but I now believe that God has chosen certain special people to do bigger and better things and the rewards are indescribable. I can see the courage in you and your wife. I can relate to her. We didn't marry you guys just for your bodies (though it may have seemed so at the time).

You'll make it, Chris, and touch many lives, just as my husband did.

Bobbi Hassenpflug
Seattle, WA

Dear Mr. and Mrs. Reeve,

I want you to know how sorry we are about the accident. In an instant our life can change and this is the reason I am writing. I want to let you know that there is hope. That miracles do happen.

In 1989, our son Lee was jogging and was hit head-on by a truck going 55 mph. Lee sustained 27 fractures in his head, his leg was severed 75 percent and he lost almost all his blood. He was to need 45 pints to live. He was in a coma and on life support. His heart stopped three times. The prognosis was that he would not survive.

So what do you do? You bring your family and friends together and you give your loved one all the support you possibly can. My husband and I took seven months off work while Lee was in rehab.

Lee is now walking, driving, attending college, golfing and working hard to get his life back to normal. It has brought our family closer. And as a board member of the Head Injury Foundation in San Diego, I have seen many patients like Lee survive and go on to have a productive and good life.

If you need any help or any questions answered, please let us know. Our prayers are with you.

Sincerely,

Lorraine and Larry Johnson

San Diego, CA

I Knew You When . . .
(1970 to 1974)

Dear Christopher,

I felt compelled to write, being someone who almost knew you. I was a freshman at Cornell, Class of '74. As you no doubt remember, those were grungy times, long before Grunge became a Seattle rock 'n' roll thing. I can still remember when I, part of the bell-bottomed, tie-dyed, frizzy-haired throng, first saw you on campus that fall of 1970. Tall, clean-cut, with those now-famous chiseled features, you seemed not to even be from the same planet as the rest of us.

You were many times that year a topic of casual conversation. Friends would mention if they shared a class with you, or had some other form of near contact, always seeming sort of surprised to have had an opportunity to share the same space with you. Let's face it, you were Different. In a good, sort of awesome way.

When word later traveled around that you had left Cornell early to go make movies, soap operas, etc., no one was ever surprised. And when, later, you were cast as Superman, my first thought was, "Well, who else could it be?" Obviously, others also seemed to feel you were from another planet—and it turned out to be Krypton.

I don't want to dwell on Superman, because you worked so hard, with so much success, to prove you were more than just a superhero.

When I entered Cornell, I didn't know where I wanted to go from there. You obviously did, and got there as soon as possible. I've always had tremendous admiration for your ability to make happen what you wanted from life.

That is why my heart goes out to you now, as you face your newest challenge. If I believed in prayers, you would be in them. But you are in my thoughts and hopes. And I wanted to let you know the impression you made upon me, even as a freshman, before your fame made an impression on so many.

Sincerely,
Deborah Addison Coburn
Silver Spring, MD

Dear Chris,

Jeez—and we thought doing . . . *Godot* was tough!

I've thought of you often over the years as you've been in the news. Usually with some regret for never thanking you properly for a post-rehearsal walk from Lincoln Hall over Fall Creek Gorge in the autumn of 1971 when you bucked me up after Peter Stelzer chastised me in front of the cast as "the laziest actor I've ever worked with." I wouldn't be surprised if you don't remember it. But I do.

How I wish I could return the favor in the face of your far

greater ordeal now. Know that I wish you all the best, and remember that you (if anyone) have the internal strength to face the challenges that lie ahead.

> Love,
> Chris Barns
> Hesperus, CO

Dear Christopher,

I want you to know I am thinking of you; I admire your courage and your spirit and I have always admired your abilities and intellect. I enclose a poem that I wrote about you.

"PERFORMANCE"
For my student Christopher Reeve

I.

I recall teaching you as Chris 25 years ago,
confident, articulate, and ambitious—
a scintillating peacock among brown wrens—
a freshman adored by magnetized young women
who dressed for your approval,
who waited to see where you would sit
before choosing their places.
Feeling the presence of Joyce, Mann, Kafka,
your mind darted sharply,
like a rainbow trout in stream,
seeking its nourishment but at times impatient
as if hurry were thought.
Bright, engaging, you bestrode
the college mindscape like a Colossus,
never quite separating performance from living.

II.

I guess when I told my sons that
I taught Superman how to fly,
you still occupied a corner of my mindscape.
It piqued my vanity's palette that you remembered me
when you thought of Cornell,

signaled me out during a visit two years ago.
I took unreasonable pride
in your public stances,
and preened myself
that in some oblique way,
I had infinitesimal influence.

III.

Who would have thought that I
a generation older
would be running and swimming
while you,
thrown from your horse,
would be saying:
"There is more to me than my body."
Vacationing far from my moorings,
walking among sea oats,
wandering on the fishing dock,
exchanging stories with folks
with whom I have only in common
the love of fishing,
and forgetting momentarily
issues of mortality,
my father's aging,
my son's efforts to find a way and a place,
sickness that becomes
common subject of conversation,
I discover your handsome smile and blue eyes
staring past Barbara Walters at me.
But between sentences you gasp, and
arm-like tubes embrace you like a mechanical octopus

enveloping an elaborate chair
designed to support muscle refuse.
Does it matter if your indomitable spirit
performs your greatest role
or if the audience is your wife, your son, yourself?

Warm regards,
Daniel R. Schwarz,
   Cornell University
Ithaca, NY

4

KIDS

The child is innocence and forgetfulness, a new beginning,
a sport, a self-propelling wheel, a first motion, a sacred Yes.

—Friedrich Nietzsche, "Of the Three Metamorphoses"

It took a week before Will could muster up the courage to walk down the corridor of 6 West—a wing in the UVA Medical Center that was serving as our home away from home—and actually enter Chris's room in the Intensive Care Unit. The last time Will had seen him, Chris was lying on a gurney, intubated, with bright caution-yellow wedges of foam stabilizing his broken neck, while the medevac helicopter waiting to take him away rumbled and whirred outside. Will had been frightened by what he saw, and I'm sure the image of his dad lying there unable to answer his questions lingered in his mind and haunted his imagination.

Matthew and Alexandra, Chris's two older children, had flown in from England with their mother and spent many hours a day with Chris—swabbing his mouth with small sponges that provided moisture and, later, when he was more fully conscious, talking to him, reading to him, kissing and hugging him. But Will, not quite three, like most children his age, probably thought that what had happened to Daddy might happen to him if he ventured too close.

So he kept his distance, listening intently to others reporting on Chris's progress, monitoring the gradually improving moods of family members. He processed the events that had occurred by acting out Chris's accident over and over on the hobby horse in the pediatrics playroom—his own self-initiated play therapy. He would fall off the horse in slow motion, calling out, "My neck! My neck!" and I would reassure him that his neck was fine, but Daddy's was injured and made it so he couldn't move.

On the day Will finally entered his father's room, Chris was wide awake, smiling, and ready to make entertaining faces. He couldn't sit up because his head was in traction and he couldn't speak due to the snugness of his newly inserted trachea tube, yet he was clearly the same Daddy in many other ways that Will recognized and loved.

We kept this first visit fairly brief, with lots of snuggling; Will chattered away about the freight trains that went by periodically outside the hospital lounge windows and the games he played with Susan and David, two kind nurses who had taken Will under their wings. (Later in the month, they would organize a little birthday party for him, complete with rubber-glove balloons and a tiny pair of scrubs gift-wrapped with a festive bow made from burn gauze.) I could see the fear melt away from Will's face as he positioned himself in the crook of Chris's motionless arm, his knobby knees resting on his daddy's belly.

We left the unit ebullient after our visit, fairly skipping past other families, other visitors who waited with familiar numb expressions brought on by worry and sleeplessness. I recognized those faces. I was one of them, on another day, perhaps. But not today.

Will's overcoming his fear had imbued him with a newfound courage. His visit had reminded Chris that his children—all of them—needed him, loved him, and delighted in him, whatever the circumstances. And I was awash in the welcome, warm glow of hope.

Will became a regular fixture in the ICU after that, learning the rules, which were strict by necessity, and befriending the hard-working, dedicated nurses. On one particular day, a short time after his first, breakthrough visit, Will sat near me on the floor of the mail room eating a small cupful of orange sherbet. The frozen treat, usually reserved for tonsillectomy patients, had been slipped to him by a newly acquired nurse friend.

"Mommy," Will said between bites of sherbet, "Daddy can't run around anymore."

"No," I replied simply. "Daddy can't run around anymore."

"And Daddy can't move his arms."

"No, he can't move his arms."

"And he can't talk."

"No. That's right—he isn't able to talk right now."

Will paused, sucked on the flat wooden spoon, his face puck-ered in concentration. And then, suddenly, brightly: "But he can still smile!"

And these are, I think, the gifts that children bring to us if we let them: hope, unadulterated love, immense courage, and the potential through any kind of hardship to still smile.

DEAR SUPERMAN,
     MY NAME IS
DANIEL NEUBAUER, I
AM 5 YEARS OLD. I
HOPE YOU GET
BETTER SOON!!!
I MISS YOU
A LOT!!!

     LOVE DANIEL

Dear Superman,

My sestrs birthday is today. I'm going to invent a poshun that will help you. I'm going to be a jyniour scientise.

Love,

Shane Matthew Morris

Charlottesville, VA

To christopher

hope you'll come out of hospital soon.

And you can come round Dad will help you up the stair's. form J.

Flying

You showing your Back

age 7 years old

Dear Superman (a.k.a. Mr. Christopher Reeve),

I hope you're okay. You're one of my biggest heroes. I mean, think about it—you started off as an unknown, now you're one of the most respected men in the world. But one thing. How did your hair get purple? Was it a wig, or did you have to dye your hair or what? I hope you feel better in the future.

Your second biggest fan (my

mom's the first),

Danny Varas

Panorama City, CA

Matt Malinsky, Tarzana, CA

Dear Mr. Christopher Reeve,

I'm sorry what happened to you. I wish you feel better soon. I like to see your Superman movies. My favorite movie was *Village of the Damned.* You are still my hero—with wheelchair or without, you are still my hero. This all I have to say.

Sincerely,

Jorge Rodriguez

Panorama City, CA

Dear Mr. Reeve,

I am 12 years old. I am like you. I am in a wheelchair. I can't walk. In Vietnam I was sick when I was three. My leg got thin.

Now I am in New Zealand. One year ago I came here to live. I had never gone to school before. Now I go to school in a taxi. I am learning to read. I go outside on my crutches at morning tea to play handball with my friends. At lunch time I go outside in my wheelchair to read books.

I go into the therapy room every morning for physiotherapy to help my muscles.

I like watching Superman. Do you think I could see you one day if I come to America?

Your friend,

Toan Tran

Auckland, New Zealand

Dear Mr. Reeve,

How are your electric pants? How are you going to celebrate Thanksgiving? I'm in second grade. Send me a picture of a salamander. Are you feeling all right?

Sincerely,

Dan Hunt

Mahwah, NJ

Finchampstead primary School,
The village,
Finchampstead,
Berkshire,
England.
7th June

Dear Christopher Reeve,
            I was sorry
to hear you had an accident.
There are so many questions to
ask but they can't be answered
not even the doctors can answer
my questions. I hope you get
well.

Love from
Holly

GET WELL

Holly Paulden, Finchhampstead, England

Dear Mr. Reeve,

I heard about your accident. I am so sorry. You don't really know me but I know a lot about you. I've seen all four of your [Superman] movies. I was wondering if we could be pen pals.

Sincerely,
Janet L. Jackson
Lynchburg, VA

P.S.: I am not the real Janet Jackson.
P.P.S.: Get well soon.

Dear Christopher,

I'm sorry that you fell off your horse. Let's hope it won't happen again.

Get well!

Sincerely,
Billy Sullivan
Santa Cruz, CA

Dear Mr. Reeve,

I am a Vietnamese boy and I got polio when I was five years old. My uncle had to carry me everywhere because I didn't have a wheelchair. Now I'm in New Zealand. I now have a wheelchair.

I came here because [we hoped] they might be able to help me walk again. Now I know that they can't help me walk, but I can do some things really well, like drawing, computer, singing and woodwork.

First I watched the TV news and I heard that you fell off your horse, and I felt sorry for you. I go to horse riding and I can go by myself. I can trot with my horse. I watched your Superman film. I really liked it. I wish you could walk again. Do you like to sit in the wheelchair?

Your friend,

Huy Do

Auckland, New Zealand

 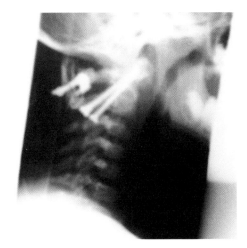

Dear Mr. Reeve,

i heard about your accident and im sorry. i broke my neck too. i had to have surgery. im ok now. i hope you will be too.

Dirk McMillan

Missoula, MT

Dear Batman,

Sister Vianney is typing this letter for me. I live in the "Holy Cross Home" because all my people are dead, and nobody wants me. I am a black boy, a Xhosa, from the Transkei. I am in grade four.

We Holy Cross children watched you acting and flying for years—you were our star. Then suddenly you disappeared, and Sister Imelda told us that you had a horse accident. Oh, we were so sorry.

I just want to tell you that we Home children pray for you every night, and we know that God will make you better and that you will be able to act again. Even the girls love you. Batman, my father, please get well. We miss you.

Please answer my letter so that we can know if you are getting better, because no one could fly like you—we want you back.

God bless and cure you.

> Your worried children of the
> H.C. Home,
> L.
> Pretoria, South Africa

Dear Christopher Reeve,

I am sorry you had a serious accident. I hope you don't feel bad. But the earth is full of reasons why you should feel glad.

> Feel better,
> Emily Mark
> Haymarket, VA

Dear Superman,

Get well soon. And may have more movies of Superman!

> From,
> H. (age 6)
> Bangkok, Thailand

Bailey Nakano, Oceanside, CA

Dear Super man,

I'm sorry that you are hert from falling off your horse. how long will you be hert? because I know how it feels to be hert. Get well.

From,
Bailey Nakano
Oceanside, CA

Dear Christopher Reeve,

Hello, I am in seventh grade at Unionville Middle School. I have always wanted to write to you because when I was little Superman was my hero. To me, you will always be Superman.

I hope very much that this letter might somehow cheer you up, even in the slightest way. You have a lot to be proud of. The most important and significant thing you can be proud of is what you did for children like me. You created a character that I could admire and look up to, as can millions of other young children. You, Superman, can be a hero for children for years to come. And nothing, no accident, can ever take that away.

Your friend,
Kelly Engel
Kennett Square, PA

P.S.: Thank you.

Dear Super man,

I hope you get better.

Sincerely,
Daryl Suyat
Oceanside, CA

Dear Mr. Reeve,

I am 9 years old and in the fourth grade. I am probably your biggest fan. I saw all four Superman movies. At school we are making a memories book. One was: Christopher Reeve (they put "Reeves," but I corrected them!) is paralyzed. My friends at school know who you are, but I don't think they're humongous, colossal, titanic, gigantic fans of yours, like me. Oh, I won the last fourth grade spelling bee. I won against the girl who won all of the spelling bees this year.

My birthday is coming up. What I want most for my birthday is for you to get better. And I forgot to mention you're my idol. I drew you, and I'm sending the drawing to you. Please, please, please get better.

Your young fan,
Gene Giannotta
Schaumburg, IL

I Knew You When . . .
(1974 to 1979)

Dear Christopher R.,

News of your accident hit me very close. I feel I discovered you myself, in Boston in 1975. I braved a Christmas-time snowstorm to see Katharine Hepburn—and you, as it turned out—in that Broadway-bound play. You were a tremendous surprise! I don't know if I'd ever heard your name before. I can't even recall the name of the play [*A Matter of Gravity*]. What I haven't forgotten is you!

What I loved immediately in that play was how your personality came through your face—playful, impish, sort of. I was telling someone this weekend how proprietary I feel about you and your smile and how stunned I was at the news of your accident; it felt personal to me.

I suddenly knew I had to write you. Despite whatever you are challenged to overcome, whatever you must accept, what I've loved about you for 20 years is still there, somewhere, if not right on top! Hold onto it. It will serve you well.

Fond wishes to you, Chris,
Mary Skousgaard
Auburn, MA

Dear Chris,

I know we haven't stayed that close over the years but I'll never forget sharing that house in the valley during the filming of *Gray Lady Down* and all the natural disasters we caused. There was the time you were cooking English muffins in the stove and neglected them for a while. I walked into the kitchen and through the haze of burnt bread I opened the stove door and found two small black briquettes. I called out, "Chris, I think your muffins are ready!"

I'm sure you'll recall walking the German shepherd (what was that dog's name—Himmler?), owned by the people for whom we were house-sitting, and watching in horror as he chomped down on one of the neighbors. Did you know that little f—— bit me the first time we walked into that house?

Gray Lady was, of course, our debut picture, and every once in a while it comes on TV. I remember you practicing your lines at night, making tortured choices between one line delivery or another as only a young actor can. You looked pretty dashing back then. Whereas I looked like a refugee from the potato famine in Ireland.

Another memory is a bit more recent: It's of me and Bonnie [Raitt] coming up to do the benefit for you in New York. It was great to be of service and even greater to have done it with you. Come to think of it, maybe we're closer than I originally thought.

And now we're both entering our forties with new challenges to face—only mine seem dwarfed in comparison with what life has dealt you. What I really want you to know is I love you and hope you can meet this part of life head on and struggle through to a place of acceptance that you, Dana, and your family can live with.

Hang tough, man! They may have jerked around with your

power lines but there are ways of reconnecting that neither you or I ever imagined. The deepest waters are, as someone once said, sometimes still.

All my love,
Michael O'Keefe
Los Angeles, CA

Dear Christopher,

I met you many years ago in New York City before you began the filming of your first Superman movie. I was working for [an eyeglass frame shop] on Madison Avenue when you and your agent came into the store. I was the optician who fit and designed the "Clark Kent" glasses for you. I remember you being very shy and polite, and I wondered if this unobtrusive young man would ever be a big movie star. Since then, I have watched your career with quiet admiration.

I only wish the best for you and pray that all of the love and encouragement you receive will help you through your most difficult times.

Sincerely,
Ellen Savage Honeycutt
Adams, TN

Dear Chris,

It has been so many years since I last saw you, but have often thought about you and how you were doing. Now, since your accident, I find myself thinking about you all the time—inspired by your inner strength and vision.

I just remembered a time, right before your first Superman movie opened, and you were visiting us at the old house on Ivy

Lane across from the [Princeton] football stadium. You and I were sitting on the front steps, looking across at the stadium's ivy-strangled walls. You said something about how you knew you were about to enter a completely different sense of reality—as if it were the quiet before the storm of public fame and recognition.

It left an impression, because there was something in the way you were sitting there and that gesture you made with your arms, sort of flinging them out toward the open air, and the open U of the empty stadium, that was exactly analogous with what you were saying about moving from a private to a very public life.

You have lived your public life to such a moral degree and set such an example—you have truly succeeded, Chris . . .

> With fond regards,
> Alastair Gordon
> Princeton, NJ

5

THOUGHTS
AND PRAYERS

God is like a mirror. The mirror never changes,
but everybody who looks at it sees something different.

—Rabbi Harold Kushner

"You want a miracle? You make a fish from scratch!"

—Larry Gelbart, *Oh God!*, spoken by George Burns
as the title character

Chris and I don't practice any traditional, organized religion and yet we remain unflaggingly spiritual in many ways. The accident, however, put our convictions to the test.

There is nothing like sudden, tragic loss to make one re-examine one's spirituality. In our case, we felt the need to reconcile somehow our belief in justice, a higher power, and the existence of a definable "goodness" with the feeling that we had somehow been betrayed. We are good people. Why had we been punished in this way? Surely there were others in the world who were arguably *not* good people—and yet they thrived.

We found tremendous comfort and wisdom in Rabbi Harold Kushner's book *When Bad Things Happen to Good People.* Neither of us believe that Chris's accident happened "for a reason," as if part of some divine plan. Rather, we accept the fact that sometimes *random* things happen to good people. Yet we have learned that we can nurture goodness and offer something to the world by how we handle our loss and by what we give to others in the process.

Love helps tremendously. Love is our religion, I guess—manifested in the deep love and understanding that Chris and I share as well as the love we give to and receive from others.

The letters in this chapter express an extraordinary commitment to love and represent an amazingly wide variety of faiths. I've come to appreciate all of the letters in their differences, and yet I am most profoundly moved by their sameness. However it is conveyed, each one bears a common sentiment: "We're rooting for you Chris. You are in our thoughts and prayers."

Dear Chris,

I was talking to Susan Sarandon yesterday, who was leaving to go see you, and it tipped me over the edge to write because I have had you in my heart so intensely ever since the Big Turning Point in your life. "God help Chris," I say, as my heart moves with you through the day and, especially, as night falls.

I keep thinking about you—that you exemplify the essence of humanness. You think, you feel, you love, you learn, you choose. The very fact of your existence, that you are, calls each of us to become more fully our essential selves. Your very being is an invitation to purification and truthfulness.

It struck me that you could conduct a unique series of interviews with people—your very presence would prompt others to a truthfulness and intimacy they would withhold from a "regular" journalist. You could talk to the poor and disenfranchised, the wealthy and powerful. I remember hearing about a play called *The Lamp*. [When the lamp was] on and people stood near it they began to tell the truth. You're like that lamp, Chris.

I'm enclosing a copy of *Dead Man Walking*. All of the experiences recorded in this book happened to me because I got involved with poor people and their struggles. As you know, Susan and Tim Robbins have made a film of my story—a very powerful film.

My love and prayers follow you, Chris.

Courage! We need you,
Sister Helen Prejean
New Orleans, LA

Dear Christopher,

As I said my prayers on May 15, I ended them the same way as always: I asked God if I've forgotten anyone, or if there is anyone He wants me to pray for. I couldn't imagine why a favorite actor's name would come to mind, but I prayed for you every night.

Weeks later when you suffered your accident, I admit I was chilled. I know God will give you the strength and courage needed for your return to health. I believe that. I'll be happy when I see that endearing smile again, right below your beautiful blue eyes.

Love and prayers,
Mary Jo Salfai
Menominee, MI

Dear Mr. Reeve,

Twenty-five years ago when we lost my 11-year-old step-daughter, tragically, a minister friend sent us the following: "I don't believe God willed this to happen, but I do believe He willed that something creative come out of it."

At the time, any message with religious overtones was off-putting; nevertheless, I found the words comforting. I hope you will also.

Sincerely,
Jackie Levering Sullivan
Claremont, CA

Dear Christopher Reeve,

Enclosed please find a medal of St. Ann. She is the reason I am writing to you. I am a retired private-school teacher, mother of two, grandmother of two and wife of 48 years to a sweet Irishman. I never knew about St. Ann until I had open-heart surgery three years ago.

I received a mass card from the St. Ann Shrine and five medals. (I don't know why!) A few days later a dear friend called to tell me she had cancer and was to take six chemo treatments. Halfway through she was not doing well, so I sent her a medal. Ten months later she called and told me she was completely cured. The doctors couldn't believe the x-rays and found no trace of the disease. (I don't know why.)

My second medal was given to a 35-year-old heroin addict who went into treatment and is now living a drug-free life. (I don't know why.)

Now my third medal is for you. Something just tells me this is where it should go. Take care and keep St. Ann with you. I'll be watching to see how you're doing. In case you're of another faith—St. Ann is Jesus' grandmother. It never hurts to have a grandmother on your side.

> Hakuna matata,
> Jacqueline Higgins
> Plantation, FL

Dear Chris,

I'm not sure how many cards you receive that are mailed to you on Yom Kippur, the holiest day in Judaism! However, I thought of you today, as I have during many of the days over this past year. Today we pray that God inscribes us all in the Book of Life, so that we may have another year of joy, happiness and health. Along with Beth, my wife, and my two boys, we are wishing you a *wonderful* New Year!

> Fondly,
> Robbie Kraft
> Encino, CA

Dear Mr. Reeve,

Hello! I learned of your accident a few days ago. I pray to God for your good health and for your return to the Original as soon as possible.

Repeat this "om" in your heart with respect and belief, and you can achieve everything you want and surely get peace.

> Luv,
> S.
> Delhi, India

Dear Chris:

Good things sometimes spring from unexpected sources—these flowers [pictured on the card], for example, growing in the rocks—

There is such an outpouring of love for you here: This afternoon, a bunch of us are meeting at 4:00 at the Congregational Church to pray for you—that healing will come in every way, beyond probability, even beyond possibility! It can! It will!

Love,
Helen Kelly
Williamstown, MA

Hi Chris,

The last time I wrote a letter in English was many years ago, so please excuse my writing. I am not a fan, just a friend unknown who wishes to help. I feel there is hope for you. The aid you most urgently need will be channeling with the "star friends." Please believe me for this is very real. You have to count on your friends from the Universe. Call them angels if you wish.

I am a very simple person, a gym teacher in Brazil. Our family has gone through many hardships. Then seven years ago I had a spiritual encounter, my life changed, and I learned much about God, life and the Universe.

Around our planet today there is a fleet of volunteers from faraway places in the Universe. They cannot be seen or detected for they are positioned in a fourth dimension of time. This fleet, known by the name of Commando Ashtar, has nothing to do with flying saucers or alien encounters. They are only endeavored to Jesus (known in the Universe as Sananda) and they are here on a mission of love. They are not invaders, but here on a rescue operation, to help prepare for the second coming of Christ.

The angels know about you. Please accept their desire to help. What is still impossible with our medicines and science is not with theirs.

You can mentally contact them through this code—"The Supreme Command of Ashtar Sheran, Archangel Michael, MX3 K20 ARCON 4229 4150." (Say your name and tell your story.) "Request assistance through code treatment 2229. Close contact by 74327."

The first signs of proof that contact has been established—a feeling of peace, "nearness," protection and shivers, which is the physical sign of contact (goose pimples). You have nothing to lose, do you? Count on your star friends, Chris. And Superman will fly again.

I'm with you, my friend,
Joao Carlos Boaventura
Barueri, Brazil

Dear Mr. Reeve,

I practice the Native American faith. You'll see on this card an elk (a symbol of stamina), bear (introspection), crow (omen of change) and owl (total truth). I pray to the Great Spirit and know you'll be back on your feet again.

Howard Dukor
San Francisco, CA

Dear Mr. Reeve,

Being an enclosed, contemplative Benedictine nun, I don't usually write fan letters to movie stars, but I'm making an exception in your case. This isn't really a "fan letter," anyway. It's more a note to let you know that you are being prayed for. You are very much appreciated by many of the Sisters in my community. We don't get to see movies very often, but we have seen at least three of yours and have enjoyed them very much.

May the Lord bless you and fill you with his healing Spirit of Love, Joy and Peace. Praying for a quick recovery. Do come and visit the next time you're in Massachusetts!

Sincerely yours,

Sr. Mary Joseph, O.S.B.

Petersham, MA

Dear Christopher,

I've had an overwhelming desire to write to you. I am not a fanatic, just a Baptist! I was born and raised in Texas. I would like to share some Bible scripture with you, and to let you know that God is with you if you ask him. It is that simple.

I hope you have a Bible: Isaiah 60:1–10; St. John 14:1–31; Psalms 29:1–11; and my favorite verse of all—Malachi 4:2—"But unto you that fear my name [Jesus] shall the sun of righteousness arise with healing in his wings; and ye shall go forth, and grow up as calves of the stall."

God has a purpose for you. I pray that you have your miracle and, in it, I pray that you know the Lord that comes with healing in His wings.

In His love,

P.

Corsicana, TX

Dear Mr. Reeve,

I, along with many others, am chanting *Nam myoho renge kyo* from the bottom of my heart for your health and your family. My Buddhist practice has helped me to live a full life, and I am confident that you will overcome this obstacle and continue to inspire the world.

Tara Kabir and the students of the
Agnor-Hurt Elementary
Afterschool Enrichment
Program
Charlottesville, VA

Dear Chris—

I have been so struck by the impact your accident has had on people everywhere. People have such admiration for your accomplishments—and this goes so very far beyond the Superman thing—but it is always followed up by a sort of incredulous "and he's such a nice person, too." As though this combination of talent, intelligence, perseverance and goodness (okay, and looks as well) could never occur in one person.

But they have, and people have not missed it. I believe that is why so many different people have been praying for you, reaching out and following you on the path to rehabilitation. You are extraordinary and your contribution, while great so far, is in a way just beginning.

Obviously, your main job right now is to get better. I am sure there will be moments of anger and frustration at what you have lost. But I believe you will find a new spirituality, a sense of wonder for what you do have, and a deep understanding of this new path that will allow you to profoundly impact those around you.

I was raised Episcopalian, [but am not] terribly religious in an organized sense. Yet I have been more than a little intrigued by the forces of spirituality, or God, that exist around us all the time and from which we can learn to draw strength. It seems to me that [your accident] has forced you into this new realm. I'm not sure what my point is; it's just that somewhere deep down I believe it will turn out very well for you.

Rest well, Chris—
Nancy Newcomer Vick
Bedford, NY

Dear Christopher,

I want you to know that we pray for you every day. Our Lord and all the saints are around you during your tribulations. I always pray to the unknown saints. I figure they are grateful for the work!

My hope is that everyone's prayers will flood your mind, heart and body with the strength you need to fight this tragedy.

Love,
Mary Louise Pullano
Skokie, IL

Dear Christopher,

I know it's hard to comfort you from where youre at but I want to asure you that there is hope. Very shortly a great and wonderful time on this planet is about to happen. Many mericales and marvelous things are going to take place. The blind will see, the deaf will hear and those who can't walk will walk again.

You may think I'm a crazy finatic who can't spell. It doesn't matter. So when you see a great sign over the Midwest you will know that all is about to happen. The awakening is almost here.

The Lord be with you,
Deb Welch
Wichita, KS

MARIANNE WILLIAMSON

October 2, 1995

Dear Christopher Reeve,

I was very moved by your interview with Barbara Walters. Thank you so much for your depth and vulnerability. I think you did more on that program to expand the minds of millions, than you did in any of your previous professional endeavors. You accomplished much.

I have been thinking about you all day, and wanted to share this thought with you: You said during the inteview that you had been the "custodian" of the Superman icon for the 70s and 80s. It occurs to me that you are much more than that.

Superman, I'm sure you realize, is a Christ figure. He who is Fathered by one who is not of this world, retains the power of his Father while living in this one. Superman is a powerful archetype, suggesting as it does to the unconscious mind that through connection to the Father, we rise above the limitations of this world. I think you chose in this life to do more than be the custodian of Superman; I think you chose to become his embodiment.

And I think you will. It was obvious, listening to you, that you have chosen the path of love and resurrection and transcendence. The power of your decision will free your mind, and in time it will free your body as well. You literally take millions with you, as you demonstrate through your own spiritual power a path of overcoming darkness.

I join all the millions who pray for you. You're a precious soul.

My love to your family,

Marianne Williamson

Dear Mr. Reeve,

[I was told] that my book *When Bad Things Happen to Good People* was helpful to you and your wife in coming to terms with your injury and your bafflement as to why a good God would let this happen to you. I was deeply moved, as I have been moved by the example you have set in coping with this monstrous misfortune. There are few feelings more sustaining than when someone tells you that your book changed their life. I believe we are here on earth to change people's lives for the better, to give hope to the despairing and courage to the faltering. I believe that God, who did not cause my son's fatal illness, showed me how to turn that illness into an instrument of redemption, and that God, who did not will or cause your accident, is doing something similar for you. I hope you are finding out how much help your life can be to others.

Please know that you are in my prayers.

Sincerely,

Rabbi Harold S. Kushner

Natick, MA

Dearest Christopher:

You have really been on my mind! I am there with you in spirit . . . helping you heal with continual energy transmissions and prayers.

Christopher . . . *there is nothing impossible!* You know that! I have been with psychic surgeons in Brazil that demolecularize tumors in 40 seconds with their *eyes.* One of these incredible healers gave me a new spinal column in 1986 after a terrible automobile accident.

Unfortunately, this healer was kidnapped, then escaped, thank God, from someone rich and powerful who wanted the healing. The healer has since kept out of touch, but I could [contact] him in Brazil so you could see him. His healings only take a few minutes.

I am a clairvoyant psychic who has an additional gift from God—I read the Akashic Records. I never look into these "soul records" without permission. But even though I have not accessed yours, I know that what you are going through is *temporary.*

Your smile has warmed my heart time and again. Your movie *Somewhere in Time* has some similarities to my own book, *I Will Always Be With You,* the story of a Palestinian queen from Chalcis and a Roman emperor whose love story spanned 2,000 years in two different planes of existence.

I send you love, healing and Aloha.

God bless you, dear one,

Triana Jackie Hill

Kihei, HI

Dear Mr. Reeve,

Yes, indeed, I am one of your fans! My name is Father Joe DeGrocco and I am a Catholic priest. (I don't know if you have ever received a letter from a priest before—perhaps I am the first . . . *and I'm not even asking for money!!!*)

Please be assured of my prayers and support for you. We even prayed for you by name one day at Mass shortly after your accident! So many times people come to me for advice and assistance when they are in the depths of difficulty and despair. Although I cannot offer them easy answers or "quick-fix" solutions, I can offer them a promise, one that I remind you of: *God never abandons us.* He will be with you as you forge ahead to meet the challenges of your life from now on. He will give you strength that you did not even know you had.

You have given me so much pleasure through your career that, as one of your fans, I just wanted to share a part of myself and my calling as a priest to help you through this time.

> Sincerely,
> Father Joe DeGrocco
> St. Frances de Chantal Church
> Wantagh, NY

Christopher, Christ-aFar—

> *Yah wah s'ya name, d'en*
> *yea-who-is-hid, in Th'heir*
> *Ya-GoD-a-Da-who-hid*
> *Awe-rise, pick up ya heart!*
> *F-high-da-hid*
> *F-High-Da-hid*
> *ya will-will ya; ya will-will ya*
> *go oD hall-mighty!*
> *Star-reign, th' Star-Reign!*
> *Fist-a-cuff (high mean) Christ-aFar*
> *"Take heart!" is th' battle cry of th' gods.*
> *GoD is—GoD is*
> *GoD-is-with-me*
> *GoD-is-with-me . . .*
> *Th' 'par-hooF is in th' puttin.'*
>> (my heart is with you),
>> Leo J. Janes
>> Fort Lauderdale, FL

Dear Chris and Dana:

I do hope you know what a substantial inspiration you are to so many people. I imagine it must get more than a little tiresome being an inspiration—it would be nice to be able to go back to being an ordinary (well, not so ordinary), mobile person again. Maybe that will happen—but meanwhile, the two of you have taken a little and made so much from it—and it continues to grow. That's at least one miracle.

It must be so hard sometimes to maintain hope—but hang in there, and know that many, many people are hanging in with you. They've been there since the day you were thrown from that horse. I told your mother that Superman is flying again. The paradox is that it's your vulnerability that has given you your new-found power—but how hard it is to be that vulnerable all the time. I think what is wrenching about your experience for so many total strangers is the fact that it so expresses what it is to be human.

I would welcome the chance to tell you both face to face what terrific people you are (and to listen a little, too). Meanwhile, know that you are in my prayers.

Faithfully,

Rev. Frank C. Strasburger

The Episcopal Church

at Princeton University

Princeton, NJ

6

CURES AND
RECOMMENDATIONS

*Do not worry; eat three square meals a day; say your prayers;
be courteous to your creditors; keep your digestion good;
exercise; go slow and easy. Maybe there are other things your
special case requires to make you happy; but, my friend,
these I reckon will give you a good lift.*

—Abraham Lincoln

*Nothing . . . refreshes and aids a sick man so much
as the affection of his friends.*

—Seneca the Younger (4? B.C.–A.D. 65), *The Healing Power of the Mind*

I am a doctor's daughter. In fact, I am also a doctor's granddaughter and a doctor's sister. Faith in Western medicine, it seems, is embedded in the genes in my family, and it was often a topic of dinner table conversation. Growing up, everyone in my family was always basically healthy—no major diseases or injuries to contend with, only the usual colds, flus, and the occasional stitch sewn into a forehead. As far as I knew, hospitals were places where people entered sick and came out well. But my father handled almost all of our minor bumps, bruises, and illnesses himself; there were no frantic calls to the pediatrician in the middle of the night or panicked visits to the emergency room. There seemed to be no sickness or injury that Daddy couldn't mend—calmly, kindly, and with humor. Our good health was a given—a blessing but an inalienable right—and my father was there to see to it.

After Chris's accident, all the assumed predictability of my life was turned on its end. The first thing I did when I was told the details of Chris's injury was to call my father. It was a natural, almost instinctual response. Surely he could explain to me in words that were easier to hear what was actually going on with my husband. Maybe he would say that the doctors in the emergency room in Culpeper, Virginia, were overreacting, that theirs was an alarmist response to a serious but perfectly solvable problem. Maybe Daddy could make it all better.

But my father could provide little more than consoling words. Medically, he was—just as all the physicians who treat spinal cord injuries are—at a loss. At the time of Chris's accident, there was no known cure for a spinal cord injury. Since then, the field of spinal cord injury has become one of the fastest growing areas of medical research. There are currently multiple therapies that have returned function to lab animals with severed spinal cords. It is now considered accepted knowledge that nerves in the spinal cord can be made to regenerate, bringing about a cure for paralysis. At the time of writing, it is projected that human trials in the treatment of spinal cord injury are about two to three years away. Back in 1995, however, traditional medicine could only do so much.

Then the letters started pouring in, many filled with sugges-
tions about how to treat Chris's injury, even how to cure it. We
received all manner of advice, from homespun remedies to complex, cutting-edge medical procedures. Spiritual healers offered
their services free of charge—and sometimes not so free of charge.
People sent ointments and lotions, vitamins and recipes. Some we
tried (various homeopathic remedies, Sygen, massage, energy
healing, to name a few), some we discarded, and others, well . . .
"I'm not quite sure *what* to make of that," Chris would say, smiling.

Nothing could cure Chris's paralysis—he would leave the hospital only a bit healthier than when he arrived—but many of the
therapies we tried made him *feel* better. And, effective or not, we
discovered that each recommendation had something special to
offer. Once again, the letter itself became a kind of curative. No
balm, pill, or surgery could achieve the effect that thousands of letters from well-wishers could.

I am still a staunch believer in the healing power of traditional
medicine, but there is no question that my horizons have been
broadened. Very few of the remedies people sent us were from the
world of medicine in which I grew up; most were alternative therapies. My father would probably laugh at many of them, dismiss
them with a wave of his stethoscope. And yet, upon closer exami-
nation, there are some amazing similarities among these varied
approaches. Clearly, these recommendations are offered with the
same qualities with which my father dispensed his medicine and
wisdom: kindness, humor, and love.

[There has been] some worthwhile success in regenerating the spinal cords of rats by surrounding the damaged cord ends with a peripheral myelin sheath that included intact Schwann cells.

Donna Holeman Kellers, R.N.

Summit, NJ

Please consider acupuncture as a possible therapy.

Karen Hearn

North Hollywood, CA

Dianetics auditing from the Church of Scientology will [help] bring [Chris] back. Talk to John Travolta. He knows.

Zulma Bonilla

Miami, FL

Lotion [made from] the mighty soybean . . .

Joanie Detlefsen

Mount Airy, MD

. . . Neuromuscular Massage Therapy . . .

C.

Alexandria, VA

I am a psychic counselor and clairvoyant . . . [and] am able to access information on illnesses . . . that standard medical procedures are sometimes unable to get.

Margo A. Schmidt

Lexington, MA

I have invented equipment which heals neurological damage. My work is unpublished but I have . . . brought people out of comas, reversed blindness, and gotten paralyzed nerves to work and limbs to move.

Deborah Banker, M.D.
Boulder, CO

The Avatar training . . . is very simple yet powerful, [one of several] consciousness tools [that] teach people self-healing.

Hanoch Talmor, M.D.
Gainesville, FL

I get such enormous delight and excitement from listening to jazz that I cannot resist recommending it to you.

Rice Odell
Washington, DC

The press have reported that Chris is trying to talk to you, but you can't understand him. I feel compelled to share the name of a woman . . . [who] is able to communicate telepathically with animals and people. It doesn't matter where they are, if they are awake, asleep or unconscious, or in or out of their earth suit.

Karen Berke
Novato, CA

As a holistic physician who had a personal experience with trauma, [I feel] electromagnetic therapy contributed to my recovery.

Alan M. Dattner, M.D.
North Grosvenordale, CT

If Christopher needs a blood transfusion, bone marrow transplant, anything at all, and you can't find a compatible donor, please do not hesitate to contact us. We'll fly to Charlottesville in no time at all.

> Amile Dju Ribeiro and Elvis Perez
> Guirola
> Miami, FL

One of the most solid modalities to . . . accelerate healing of fractures and injuries due to trauma . . . is called Therapeutic Touch, but it does not involve actually touching the patient.

> Frances D'Amico, Ph.D.
> Appomattox, VA

Medical technology will probably never tap into the power of mental energy, so if you're looking for another means to help yourself, I recommend *Creative Visualization,* by Shakti Gawain . . .

> Carol Empet
> Freeville, NY

. . . *A Whole New Life,* by Reynolds Price, who had a tumor of the spine . . .

> Bette Heishman
> Richmond, VA

. . . the song "Hero," by Mariah Carey.

> Ingrid Storm
> San Jose, CA

One thing that's sure to put a smile on your face— Tchaikovsky's Violin Concerto in D played by Itzhak Perlman.

> Cynthia Bonanno
> Mission Viejo, CA

I have been [conducting] absentee healing treatments [for] you going on approximately three weeks. You do not have to believe in it for it to work.

> Ralph Bland
> Mead Valley, CA

I will be glad to come to Virginia and lay hands on Christopher and pray for him.

> D.
> Marietta, GA

I juice pineapple and grapefruit for a muscle relaxer, or two apples and one celery stalk. It works. (Wash in cold water with salt and lemon juice to rid of pesticides.)

> M.
> Rockingham, NC

Add to your diet food-grade linseed oil. . . .

> R.
> Philadelphia, PA

. . . bioflavonoids, vitamin C and calcium—and one must get in sunshine for 20 minutes a day in order for the calcium to be absorbed.

> Betty Thielbar
> Boynton Beach, FL

I and my husband have both had dreams about your condition. [In my husband's dream], David was informed that LSD Psychotherapy could help heal the trauma.

Although it may seem strange to write such a letter about

healing solutions that come from complete strangers in dreams, it is not so strange. It is believed that many of the treatments for serious diseases came to the ancient Chinese acupuncturists in dreams.

The dream I had about you last night was that you were able to walk again. And I do pray that this dream comes true.

Rebecca and David Wilkinson
South Strafford, VT

Hyperbaric oxygen chambers . . . ozone therapy . . . and glandular therapies have been used for years in clinics throughout Germany and Switzerland.

Joan C. Priestley, M.D.
Anchorage, AK

. . . The use of a rocking chair helps speed the healing of wounds because of a kinetic therapy provided by the constant Gentle Motion.

Helen E. Kerchner
LaPorte, IN

Bee venom therapy is helping people with all kinds of health problems, including arthritis, multiple sclerosis, cancer, lupus, Parkinson's disease, etc. There have been some amazing results.

Marjorie Jennings
Macon, GA

Vita Fons II is a life-enhancing, energy-encoding ointment that operates on the spiritual-energy plane.

Mary-Sue Haliburton
Ottawa, Ontario, Canada

My husband is a C2, C3 quadriplegic and has been for 15 years. We were wondering if you know about phrenic nerve pacemakers. Chuck breathes with assistance from them.

Robyn Foss
Saco, ME

I have a gift of G-d in my hands where I lay my hands on a sick person and my energy flows thru and they get well very quickly. I have never healed a paralyzed person, but if you want to try my energy please contact me and I will of course need airfare and expenses. I don't charge anything if I fail.

M.

A friend of mine in Bombay has healed many thousand people by reciting prayers for a speedy healing. All you have to do is to drink half a glass of luke-warm water after brushing your teeth every morning. The water should be plain drinking water and nothing must be added. The prayers said by my friend will enter your body through the water and the healing will perhaps aston-ish your doctors . . . There is no charge for this service.

Bomi Dastoor
Pune, India

Scientists have established beyond any doubt that all living cells are electromagnetic in nature. Placing a *strong positive magnet over the spinal cord* for a few minutes on the injured area *will stimulate it.* Then by placing a strong negative magnet on the area for a longer period of time, will normalize the acid-base balance and promote healing.

Judy Loney
Milwaukie, OR

My son was right where you are last year at this time. I know how panicked a family can get—mothers especially. If any of your family needs a break, I recommend the Cloister at Sea Island, Georgia. We retired down here and love it.

Mary Baldwin

Saint Simons Island, GA

I also fell off a horse on Saturday. I was taking a lesson when my horse decided to take me for a run. I broke a transverse vertebra in my back. My cat has been a great source of comfort to me while I'm spending so much time in bed. Maybe when you get out of the hospital you could get a cat, if you don't already have one.

Jennifer Galt

Cranston, RI

. . . And honorable mention goes to: tai chi, qi gong, Norman Cousins's *Anatomy of an Illness,* a high-protein diet, Sygen, Body/Mind Empowerment therapy, *Good News for Modern Man,* myofascial release technique, pregnenolone hormone treatments, James Dobson's *When God Doesn't Make Sense,* ancient Druid meditational chiming spheres, omega-3 fatty acids, Sogyal Rinpoche's *The Tibetan Book of Living and Dying,* Charlotte Joko Beck's *Everyday Zen,* Barbara Brennan's *Light Emerging,* Norman Vincent Peale's *You Can If You Think You Can,* embryonic cell transplant therapy, ice therapy, colloidal silver, proanthocyanins, dimethyl sulfoxide anti-inflammatory treatments, blue-green algae, Zhu's Scalp Acupuncture, yoga, James Redfield's *The Celestine Prophecy,* cranial osteopathy, postsynaptic H-Reflex Wave, Octacosanol, connected breathing/rebirthing, Larry Dossey's *Healing Words,* human growth hormone, cayenne pepper, ginger, The Sam Biser Save Your Life Herbal Video Collection, chanting, audio frequency therapy, reflexology, sacro-occipital technique, Elton John's "The Circle of Life," Christian Science healing, Computerized Diaphragmatic Breathing Retraining . . . and many more.

Thank you all.

I Knew You When . . .
(1979 to 1985)

Dear Chris,

Quite a few years ago you attended the Special Olympics in Brockport, New York. I was a teacher volunteer at this event, and my "special" charge wanted to meet "Superman" in person. As you came toward us down the walk, I approached you and introduced her to you. Needless to say, I was more thrilled than she.

I remember that you were so gracious, such a gentleman and so kind to these children that my admiration for you increased ten-fold. I have never forgotten that moment.

When I heard of your accident, I was appalled. My prayers are with you.

> Sincerely,
> Joanne Quigley
> Rochester, NY

Dear Christopher,

My son, Greg Hall, was most proud to have worked with you when filming *Somewhere in Time.* As you may recall, he worked on the clothing design team and was nominated for an Academy Award.

He thoroughly enjoyed the plane trip when you piloted him and Jane Seymour from Mackinac Island to a session of bowling on the mainland. You are a man of many talents.

Sincerely,

Laura M. Hall, Mayor

Edmonds, WA

Dear Christopher:

You may not remember me but I played your wacky mother-in-law in *The Front Page* at Williamstown in 1980 (Kate Burton's mother). I wanted to remind you of your kindness to me in what was a "challenging" time for me (albeit a small challenge). I recall standing in the wings, substituting for Celeste Holm, and having you give me a hug and encouraging words: "You can do it, kid."

I've not forgotten that—a small thing, perhaps, and probably not remembered by you but it gave me the lift I needed to get the job done.

I know you have the courage and will to move through your own "challenge." I will hold you in the white light of wholeness and love, with the belief that "You can do it, kid."

With all best wishes,

Carolyn Byrne

Seattle, WA

Dear Mr. Reeve,

It was after a performance of *Fifth of July* in New York City that we spoke briefly one night. It was November, 1980, and a group of us waited at the stage door of the New Apollo Theater. It was a windy, wintry night. The doorman, noting we were freezing, invited us in so we could take shelter.

The waiting area was small. There was a metal circular stairway going up and the stage was only a few steps away from where we stood. The doorman said that Mr. Reeve would be down soon to sign our *Playbills.*

Harry and I would come into the city several times a year and always enjoyed the theater, but we had never been back-stage before. In no time at all you came down the stairs smiling and opened to us all. You have no idea how your presence filled that space. I was so awe-struck that I went completely blank and could hardly remember my own name. I mentioned we were teachers (like your father) and, when you looked at me and asked "Where do you teach?" I couldn't remember!

Thank you for being so gracious and giving me such a wonderful memory of that special night at the theater. I will never forget it.

> Sincerely,
> Ed Legutko
> Wilton, CT

Chris!

I was blown over when I heard what happened to you. I started a couple of letters but wasn't sure what to write. My mother and aunt thought I had a direct line to you. When I finally told them I knew no more about you than they did, I got blow-by-blow reports: "He's sitting at 80 degrees now!" "He's eating food!" "He's watching television!"

The folks at the neighborhood tavern read an article in the paper that explained how I worked with you [as a consultant, when you portrayed the disabled character] in the Broadway production *Fifth of July.* All the old retired sanitation men started to buy me drinks and asked "How's Chris doing?" You know what I tell them? I say "Chris is going to be fine."

No matter how bad it gets, know there is a God. Why? Because God created Pathmark. [On days when I'm down,] I get in my wheelchair, get in the car and drive to Pathmark. I park in the handicap spot like a diplomat. The security guard greets me at the entrance. I take my time, go up and down the aisles, talk to people. There's nice music. What more do I want out of life?

I had a friend who was a bookie, a big time gambler. It was a family thing. His aunts ran the numbers for years. If you wanted anything—TV's stereos, food, furniture, anything—he could get it for you. You'd have to park your car a block away and pick it up at 4:00 in the morning, but he could get it for you. The guy's name was Iggy.

Anyway, he got in a fight in Atlantic City and someone threw him down a flight of stairs. Iggy was now going to be in a wheelchair for some time to come. After a couple of years, Iggy got back to Atlantic City. As one would expect, he could still get you anything you needed. You still have to park a block away and pick it up at 4:00 am, but Iggy'll be there for you.

He told me once how he felt about his physical situation. He said, "God is up there with a deck of cards. He deals them out not by what you deserve but what you can handle. He's not going to give some yo-yo something traumatic to handle. God'll deal the tough hands to those who can take it, to those who can do something with it."

You know it's going to be tough, Chris. I know it's going to be tough. Everyone knows. But I feel you can handle it. You got enough people praying for you. My mother and my cheap aunt lit a candle for you. You can't ask for more than that.

Best,
Mike Sulsona
Staten Island, NY

I am so sorry to hear of your accident. I met you a few times on the Rexall lot in L.A. (I'm the parking attendant). My wife and I wish for you a complete recovery.

>Sincerely,
>Al and Lenore Bass
>Los Angeles, CA

Dear Mr. Reeve,

About 12 years ago my best friend's son, John Beebe, died of cancer of the spine on Long Island. He was 18 years old. His dying wish was to spend some time with you, and somehow word was passed on to you. In spite of your busy schedule, you managed to spend several hours visiting with John and helping to make his final days a little happier.

You have had a special place in the hearts of my entire family ever since. This sort of quiet kindness on the part of celebrities is probably more common than the average person suspects. Occasionally we read about such acts, but when they happen to someone we know and there is no publicity, the humanity of the celebrity becomes that much more special.

It is heartening to hear that your condition is improving a little each day. I am sure that if a generous nature counts for anything in the scheme of things, you will be well very soon.

>Sincerely,
>Bruce L. Follmer
>Alexandria, VA

Dear Chris,

You may not remember my name, but I knew you in London in 1985 when [your son] Matthew was five and in the same school as the boy I was looking after. My favorite memory is of Matthew's fifth birthday party, when you opened a second bottle of champagne, saying, "What the hell, you only turn five once!"

It is that spirit that I hope can sustain you now when you need it the most.

With affection,

L.

Dear Chris,

One Sunday morning at 72nd Street and Broadway years ago, I was driving a gypsy cab—you got in and asked, "How much to Teterboro Airport?" I said, "$15," you said "I'll give you $30." Thanks.

C. Christopher Compton
North Hollywood, CA

Mr. Reeve,

This note of thanks is many years overdue. I only wish I could return the comfort and compassion you showed me.

It was about 10 years ago, in Martha's Vineyard. I was traveling alone and was involved in a moped accident. I remember a hand on my shoulder as I attempted to stand up, your hand, trying to guide me back down. I hadn't seen your face, only heard your voice, "Sit, you don't know how hurt you might be." I started shaking and turned to face you. It was almost comical. I wondered if maybe I had died—that maybe there was no God—that maybe instead of St. Peter—Superman really did exist.

It is easy to recall the concern in your eyes, your voice yelling for someone to call an ambulance—and telling me to put my head down. You stayed with me till the police came, and even offered to go with me to the hospital. The gratitude I felt then was immeasurable—today it is never-ending.

Know that there is a stranger in this world who saw in your eyes a safe place. I wish for you that same vision.

Thank you for giving of yourself,

V.

7

THE PLAYING FIELDS

*The pessimist complains about the wind; the optimist expects it
to change; the realist adjusts the sails.*

—William Arthur Ward

*"Think about the day when you'll look that horse in the eye
and say, 'I'm back, you S.O.B.' "*

—V. E. Obermeier
Laurel, MD

Chris developed a passion for horses relatively late in life. Late, that
is, compared to the prepubescent obsession that many young
girls—myself included—develop in grade school. An avid, lifelong
sailor, skier, pianist, hockey player, tennis player, SCUBA diver,
and pilot (just a partial list), Chris had mastered so many things
there were few left to try. But by the time we met in the summer
of 1987, the riding bug had bit, and bit hard.

In riding, as in everything he focuses on, Chris became
extremely proficient very quickly. He was well respected as a seri-

Chris competing over fences on his horse Denver, 1993

ous and skilled horseman among the riding community and he found this recognition supremely gratifying.

Chris has a profound love for anything done well—whether it's a perfectly trimmed sail, the flawless playing of a piano concerto, or even the satisfaction derived from the seemingly more mundane achievement of a spotlessly cleaned room. (My husband has always been "the neat one," and his tolerance of my more chaotic style is, in my view, one of his greatest testaments of love for me.) A self-described "action junkie," he is someone who pushes himself to achieve the highest possible standard in everything he does, and he secretly—or sometimes not so secretly—

Piano practice with Will

expects the same of others. He is not a dabbler. In an age when the rallying cry often heard is "Whatever," his passion and commitment are a refreshing, awe-inspiring anomaly.

Chris's perseverance and high standards have not been compromised by his disability. He continues to be a visionary who expects a great deal of himself and others. But he desperately misses the hobbies and sports he so dearly loved. And truly, Chris's physical achievements are part of what have always defined him. They help comprise his very essence.

Never one for the sidelines, Chris is now forced to watch others participate in the activities that used to nourish him daily. The miracle is that he does so with patience, interest, impossible generosity, and good humor. For all his extraordinary and varied physical accomplishments, enduring stillness with grace is, I think, Chris's most difficult and courageous endeavor—a feat by far his most heroic.

Dear Mr. Reeve:

As a fellow equestrian, I know there are risks we take, but in all reality, they are ones we never want to face. When I heard in the news of your accident, it was personal for me. You are facing something that is one of the ultimate sacrifices all for the love of horses.

I have hope that your body will decide to mend. And that you will find your way back in the saddle again.

In training, there is something said that is so true in life: "Keep your head up, look for the next fence."

Sincerely,

Sarah Hussin

Milwaukee, WI

Dear Christopher Reeve,

I met you while you were riding the cross-country at the Koolah Event at Millarville, Alberta (Black Diamond Land & Cattle Co.) in 1993. I was quite impressed by the care and concern you afforded your horse after the cross-country, as it would have been very easy for a celebrity such as yourself to hand the horse over to someone else while you made yourself comfortable. (It was a very hot day.) That showed you to be a real horseman.

I am keeping you in my prayers.

Tricia Dahms
Rocky Mountain House,
Alberta, Canada

Mr. Reeve,

I happened to catch a piece of your wife's press conference, where she alluded to the fact that you are a Rangers fan. Please accept the enclosed video cassettes of the Rangers' 1994 Stanley Cup run as a gift from one formerly long-suffering Rangers fan to another. Best wishes toward your recovery.

Regards,
David Parmele
Herndon, VA

Dear Mr. Reeve:

In the 1980s it was my pleasure to provide flight services and pilot weather briefings to you (N123CR) while working at the Albany Flight Service Station. Your professionalism as a pilot was always respected.

Good luck,
Art Schehr
Saratoga Springs, NY

Chris—

You have been on my mind every day since your accident. I cleaned out your horse trailer for you, have called Carl to re-shoe Buck, had Dr. Weinburg in to check him over, and also plan to have the equine dentist see him. Until we hear from you, Buck can remain at Peace & Carrots [stables] and, of course, the trailer can remain on the property. If there is anything more I can do, don't hesitate to ask.

All my love,
Suze Rubin
Pound Ridge, NY

Dear Chris, Dana and Will,

You know, we really miss you guys. For a while there were daily updates on all the channels, but lately we haven't heard much, and that's been hard. We see Buck in his stall every day, but that's not enough . . . I'd much rather give you a carrot and an apple, frankly! Or just a big hug—God knows if you even like carrots and apples.

I enclosed a copy of the snapshot from Culpepper. Chris, it's so you and Buck—so alert, so poised. I hope you like it.

All our love,
Carla and Peter Lazare
New York, NY

Dear Christopher

Ten days before your accident, a tree fell on me and broke my back. As I went through the terrible days of early recovery my prayers have been for you as well as myself.

I know you better as a flyer than an actor, and I pray that the day will come when we both can once again "Top the windswept heights with easy grace, reach out our hand, and touch the face of God."

With hope for a speedy recovery,
Dick Grow,
    another Stearman pilot
Lake Lure, NC

Dear Chris,

Your flying buddies at the Wurtsboro Airport are wishing you a speedy recovery and an early return to sailplane flying. (It's safer!)

Best regards,
Rolf Bahrenburg
Huntington, NY

Dear Mr. Reeve,

I felt I had to write to let you know that there is someone who knows what you and your family are going through at this time. I was thrown, while exercising a racehorse, fourteen years ago, and I am paralyzed from the mid-chest down. I was a single mom with two daughters who witnessed my accident at the ages of 9 and 13. Close friends of mine were kind enough to take care of the girls for the summer so my family could be with me at the hospital.

I had been riding and showing horses for twenty-six years and my girls continued to show even after my injury. In fact, when I was finally allowed to leave the rehabilitation center on weekends I would go and watch them show and coach them on their riding technique. Many people wonder how I can continue to have interest in horses and I just tell them that it was a freak accident and you deal with it and go on. Every time you get on a horse you take a risk because they are bigger and more powerful than you are, even if you know how to fall.

From what I've been hearing on the news you definitely have a lot of support from family, friends and fans. They will be a big help to you in your recovery—but it has to come from within yourself for your recovery to be a success. Good luck, and a speedy recovery.

Sincerely,
Woodie Hunt
Zanesville, OH

Dear Chris and Dana,

School has begun here in L.A. and Faye and the kids and I seem to be settling in. It's so beautiful and pleasant that one thinks, "What's wrong with this picture?" The answer: earthquakes, floods and show-biz creepos under every rock. On the other hand, yesterday I went fly fishing with Chris Guest deep into the Angeles Forest in a secret river that we accessed by walking down a two-mile fire road. The trick is that at the end of the day you have to walk back up. Very, very up.

It's grueling in the heat, but it keeps the faint of heart away. We didn't see another human all day. Chris and a friend who joined us are expert fishermen and caught (and threw back) dozens of little rainbows (wild, not stocked). I was humbled. I got two good bites, but lost the clever little buggers. Fly casting is beautiful and so difficult.

We also found a perfect swimming hole and had an almost mystical swim: cold, cold water, but blue sky, no wind and great company. All this two hours from where I sit now. I'm trying to stay focused on the great things about L.A. and ignore the biz as much as possible. So far it's working.

I hope this finds you full of energy and love. We send more of the latter, knowing you always have plenty of the former.

Steve [Stephen Collins]
Los Angeles, CA

Dear Mr. Reeve:

It is my understanding that our "new" Swan 40, formerly known as Chandelle, once belonged to you. Knowing the relationship one has with a sailboat (past and present), I thought you might be interested to learn that she is back in the water, having rested ashore for two and a half years in a Connecticut boatyard. We shipped her to Maine last November and logged many hours on her throughout the winter. We varnished and painted, updated the plumbing and electronics, and installed the necessary modern electrical systems, among many other things.

Her new name is Chase, and her port of call is the Portland Yacht Club in Falmouth, Maine.

We launched her in Portland last Tuesday, stepped the mast on Wednesday and powered her to Falmouth. Yesterday we bent the sails, in the lee of Clapboard Island, as the wind freshened hard out of the northwest. Finally, it was time to see what she was made of . . . the old B&G windspeed indicator reading a steady 20 to 22 knots, as we smoked out into the middle of the bay around Clapboard. She loved it! She handled like a charm, stiff, stable and no weather helm, and did she move! We were alone in the bay, as the air temperature was 42 degrees and the water was 36 degrees. We were having such fun the cold spray in the face went unnoticed. We could really feel the old lady wanting to run, having lain idle for too long. It is wonderful rejuvenating this beautiful vessel and unleashing her energy.

I am told that you used to cruise the coast of Maine aboard Chase. We want you to know that, if you plan to visit Maine in the summer, we would be pleased and honored to have you sail her again.

In closing, I should like to add that your courage and attitude is an inspiration to us all. We wish you well . . . "with fair winds and following seas."

Best regards,
Gregg A. Marston
Cumberland Foreside, ME

Christopher sailing Chandelle

I Knew You When . . . (1986 to 1993)

Dear Christopher:

It's been nine years since we worked together on the movie *Street Smart* (I was the costume designer), but I will never forget you and Mimi Rogers taking me out for Mother's Day—it was so sweet of you.

I just want you to know that I pray for you and your lovely family.

> With love,
> Jo Inocencio

Dear Mr. Reeve:

In 1990 I was named deputy chairman of the National Endowment for the Arts—at the zenith of the so-called controversies. When the NEA was in big trouble, you suddenly appeared as an articulate voice in support of the arts—a member of a group we at the NEA called "The Hollywood Few." You were sophisticated enough to know that Washington responds to nudges, and understood that to take no risk was the greatest risk.

You helped us; you probably bugged Congressmen to vote for the NEA or at least shut up. And you raised the morale of my staff and arts people throughout America.

God dealt you a bad hand, but years ago He slipped you trump cards: your tenacity and intellectual talent. Oh, we wish you well!

In gratitude,
Randy McAusland
Fort Lauderdale, FL

Dear Mr. Reeve:

We shook hands once in 1988 when you were visiting my pediatric patients at Memorial Sloan-Kettering Cancer Center in New York. I will never forget the way you took the time to don hat, mask, gown, gloves and booties necessary to see the children receiving bone-marrow transplants. As you may be aware, many celebrities visit Memorial. None of the TV stars or rap musicians took the time or had the courage to "gown up" and face these unfortunate children. Even though cancer is not contagious, most of the celebrities would not touch them.

The sight of these small, bald, sick and isolated children scared most adults. The most impressive aspect of your visit (that will be with me always) was that you were not afraid to touch each child. All of the children you visited remembered your gentle touch. To them, your heroism was the action in the movies, but to me your kindness and quiet courage were more heroic than any physical stunt performed by Superman.

I wish I could gather those children and come visit you to repay the kindness. I am sure that they are with you in spirit. Recovery from an accident such as yours is a slow process and it is easy to be overwhelmed and hopeless. One of my patients once told me, "I can't give up—I don't know what fun I might miss."

Rest comfortably, and know that you have had a positive impact on many small lives, and at least one pediatrician.

With kindest wishes,

Bruce Reidenberg, M.D.

Upper Montclair, NJ

Dear Mr. Reeve,

About seven years ago you had lunch at my restaurant (a shack of an old boat house in Thomaston, Maine). The waitresses and I had all we could do to contain ourselves. As the girls said, in true Maine lingo, "He's right handsome." You just seemed like a good person. Your celebrity status didn't seem to affect your friendly and charming way with all of us.

I think about your condition every day, and truly hope you will be sailing again off the coast of Maine soon.

My thoughts are with you,

Victoria Covill, former owner

of the Harbor View Tavern

Union, ME

Dear Christopher,

I was just thinking back to [the filming of *Noises Off*], and you, Tony Shaloub, my wife, Paula Roth, and I were playing "The Poker Game" at Mark Linn-Baker's home—*which, by the way, is for sale, I have the listing, I'm a broker, it's a lovely 3+ maid's; there I go again, always trying to bring up business.* We had a good time that day. But we never got to talk about anything. We were all too busy trying to explain the rules of those crazy card games we wanted to play. The last hand we played that day was my strange game that, as I recall, you won. And it was a mighty big pot.

But if we were sitting next to one another today, I would forgo the crazy poker games for a minute and tell you about the time I fell off the roof. It was 20 years ago. I was a mess. Half the experts said I was paralyzed for life, half said "Let's wait and see." Well, eventually I did get my feeling back and learned to walk again. Today, I can play poker with the best of them.

I learned then that we are all dealt our hand in life. And we just have to play it out and make the best of it. Some get good cards, others bad. The extremes are the healthy children born to wealthy parents, and babies born with physical and mental handicaps that can't be fixed. And sometimes, especially in some of those wild seven-card games we played, a good hand can, after three or four cards, turn to, well, not such a good hand. Play it out, Christopher. You have family and friends who want you to be a part of their lives.

Until our next game, I wish you luck,
Carl Scheinwald
Woodland Hills, CA

Dear Mr. Reeve,

Meeting you four years ago in the Hard Rock Cafe was the most exciting thing that ever happened to me in my life. I always wanted to thank you. You have been my idol for such a long time and helped me get through my illness. I wish there was something I could do to help you feel better. I know that hospital is not the place anyone wants to be in, but it is not that bad. I practically lived in hospitals for two years, when I had bone marrow transplant. Please don't give up. Be strong and hang in there.

Sincerely,
Sean Hannes
Elgin, IL

(We met Sean at the Hard Rock Cafe the day Chris and I told Matthew and Alexandra that we were getting married.)

Dear Chris and Dana,

There are moments when a person enters your life and leaves a lasting impression. Such was the case when, as a crew member aboard the Schooner Zodiac, I had the rare pleasure of working with Chris on the film *The Sea Wolf.* During the shoot I was stationed at the helm.

The first two days, between scenes, you noted the strong winds, took the helm and did what we crew members love to do— sail really, really fast. A love, I fear, not shared by as many cast and crew members, given the high number of bodies hanging over the rail. A record, I believe, that you still hold, and a beloved addition to Zodiac folklore.

You were a godsend during the shoot, Chris, acting as a go-between for the director and the ship's captain. Your professionalism was absolute, and the ship's crew would not have made it through without you. Thank you.

> Know that my thoughts are with
> you all,
> A.

Christopher and Matthew sailing the schooner Zodiac

8

BACKSTAGE

Everyone wants to feel that they belong—that they are respected, admired, and loved by their peers. When Chris had his accident, the film and theatrical communities in Hollywood and New York responded so quickly and with such unmitigated love and support that Chris and I both felt part of an enormous, giving family.

Chris received scores of messages, notes, and telegrams from fellow artists: actors on location overseas, entire Broadway casts, production companies, film and television crews. Many friends and colleagues also came to visit throughout the long months in rehab and after. Chris had the unique and rare opportunity to be shown during his lifetime how many friends he has and how much they care.

As is the case in other parts of this book, most of the correspondence we received from celebrity friends and colleagues cannot be included because of the sheer volume of it. These letters remain carefully tucked away. At this point I feel compelled to confess that, regrettably, some were *too* carefully tucked away. In fact, they seem to have been tucked right into oblivion.

Among "The Lost Letters" were sweet and funny messages from Susan Sarandon, Blair Brown, Richard Donner, and—you're just going to have to trust me on this one—a priceless quip from Woody Allen.

The misplaced letter I am the saddest about, however, is the one from Princess Diana, delivered via Barbara Walters in 1996. It was a handwritten note on ivory paper with a blue cursive "D" on the letterhead. Diana spoke eloquently about her admiration for Chris's courage and she recalled a time when they had once danced together, expressing hopes that one day they would dance together again.

He would have liked that.

Katharine Houghton Hepburn

IX - 21 - 1995

Dear Christopher -

     - Let me know if I can do
anything - My golly what a mess -

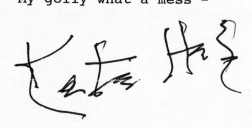

Dear Dana & Chris—

The [Barbara Walters] interview was extraordinary. All through it I kept saying to myself—what a comfort and inspiration you are and will continue to be for our poor fractured country. You spoke directly to everyone's heart and soul. You both were radiant and articulate and deeply, deeply moving. You are constantly in my thoughts and prayers.

> Love,
> Glennie [Glenn Close]
> Actor

Dearest Christopher,

Just a short note to let you know we are all thinking of you—praying *very, very hard* for you. You have so many who love you and are sure you will be triumphant—God Bless.

> We send love—
> Maria, Arnold & family
>   [broadcast journalist Maria
>   Shriver and actor Arnold
>   Schwarzenegger]

Dear Chris,

Please know that you have my deepest concern and good wishes. If it's alright with you, I would very much like to come for a visit in the near future. In the meantime, if there is anything I can do . . .

> Best regards,
> John Travolta
> Actor

Cecilia & James Earl Jones

13 June '95

Dear Christopher,

  If kisses really can "make it all better", we want you to know we're sitting here all puckered up.

  Love,
  Ceci & James Earl Jones

My darling Christopher,

I do not know when this may reach you but I must write to you—I am near the places we were when filming *Remains of the Day*—in the west country—and heard of your accident through the press. I hoped against hope that the reports were sensationalized but it seems certain now that you are gravely injured. I cannot help but cry as I write this, which is hopeless and useless of me.

You cannot imagine with what love and hope I think of you and Dana and the children. I hold you all constantly in my heart, my thoughts and in my strange secular prayers.

I do not know what you must be feeling or thinking—all I am certain of is that it is the best of men, the most loving and generous and kind, whom life has changed in this way. Whatever you do, or think, or feel, comes from such a very noble spirit that will touch everyone around it. Of this I am certain.

Not everything is expressible in words and I think you know the feelings that come with this.

> All my love, dearest,
> Emma [Emma Thompson]
> Actor and screenwriter

My dear Christopher:

On behalf of all those in "Hollyweird" who care about you, I want to wish you the speediest of recoveries and let you know that we are thinking about you.

> With lots of love and the greatest
> of affection,
> David [David Niven, Jr.]
> Producer

HEAL!

PENN & TELLER

Dear Chris,

We think about you so much. I've been casting the Picasso film in a room at Warner Bros. on 54th Street, and on the wall behind me is a very large black-and-white print of you flying straight toward the camera in *Superman*. All the actors see it—how can they not? The picture dominates the room. You seem a bit like a protective angel. And lately—before your accident—it did seem that all the public work you were doing had a protective quality. You flew down to right wrongs. So the image of you lying all sort of broken on the ground is a hard one to imagine.

But what is not hard to imagine is your powerful will and resolve that are still intact, and everyone—friend or stranger—

who sends you greetings and prayers is agreed that if anyone should make it back from such a disaster it will be you. So you see, whatever you do, we all can't help thinking of you as invincible and indestructible.

With much love always,

Jim and Ismail [James F. Ivory and

Ismail Merchant]

Filmmakers

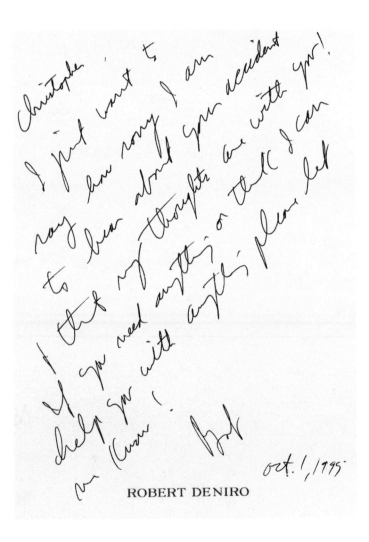

ROBERT DENIRO

Dear Chris,

Every time we pick up a paper and read even more encouraging news, it makes us realize that what made it easy for us to write [screenplays about the] hero character [Superman] is that you are our real-life hero.

Incidentally, last week our son and his wife presented us with our first grandchild—a girl—so now you have one more human being on Earth rooting for you.

All our love,
David and Leslie Newman
Screenwriters, *Superman I, II, III*

Chris—

I'm thinking of you.

Love,
Whoopi [Whoopi Goldberg]
Actor

My dear Christopher Reeve,

Well it is about time I wrote to you! I hope you remember me, we used to see each other at the ferry boat from Martha's Vineyard. I remember always thinking how fabulously beautiful you are when I would see you there.

I certainly can sympathize with your circumstances as I found myself in a somewhat similar situation when I suffered three strokes shortly after receiving the Academy Award in 1964. After many years of rehabilitation it is still with me and always will be. I have found comfort over the years in assisting others afflicted with my disease and, in fact, even have a hospital named after me in my hometown of Knoxville, Tennessee.

I wish you every success, you courageous man! I would love to take you and your divine wife to dinner whenever possible. Until we meet . . .

> With great admiration,
> Patricia Neal
> Actor

RICHARD DREYFUSS

June 12, 1995

Dear Chris:

I have neither the facility nor the experience to give you any wisdom except my love.

Dear Christopher,

All the Kennedys and their offspring are praying for your speedy recovery. You have done so much for us through the years and we certainly need you now and in the future. We send much love to you and your family.

Pat Kennedy Lawford

Christopher Reeve:

Thinking of you with all of our love.

Antonio Banderas and Melanie
Griffith
Actors

Dear Chris and Dana,

We so wish there was some way we could help you in your endeavors. You are both so articulate and empowering to so many people who have no idea what you must be going through. You will make a huge difference to our world as we know it. If we can ever help you, please call us. If we can see you, too, please let us know. We miss you and love you.

All our love,
Jane and James [Jane Seymour and
James Keach]
Actor and director

P.S.: We are going to name one of our twin boys Christopher—after you.

Dear Chris,

I just want to add one more voice to the zillions who I'm sure have written and called you and your family. You and I worked together in the 1980 Williamstown season—we did *The Front Page,* and I was your understudy in *The Cherry Orchard.* (You once had to fly to New York to do the *Today* show, missing rehearsal and leaving me as your understudy to face Colleen Dewhurst all by myself— I've never forgiven you.)

Fate has handed you, your family and your friends a tough one with this accident; today I read in the paper that your breathing requires support. Well, you have it, because every one of your friends, colleagues and fans is breathing right along with you.

> Sincerely,
> David Hyde Pierce
> Actor

Dear Christopher,

Do you remember our meeting at the Haymarket [Theater] long ago? Was I giving you a prize or were you giving me one? You must be sick and tired of being praised for your incredibly deter-mined refusal to accept defeat after your unhappy accident. I send you my sincerest good wishes.

> Very sincerely,
> John Gielgud
> Actor

Dear Chris and Dana—

Do you know what you two have done for this country? Brought out all its slumbering humanity and caring. You're both remarkable!

> Love,
> Blythe D. [Blythe Danner]
> Actor

JUNE 2ND, 1995

ATTENTION: CHRISTOPHER REEVE
UNIVERSITY OF VIRGINIA MEDICAL CENTER
CHARLOTTESVILLE, VIRGINIA 22908

DEAR CHRISTOPHER,

YOU'RE A PRINCE TO THE WORLD IN THE WAY OF ECOLOGY AND HAVE MAINTAINED A
LEVEL OF CHARM AND GRACE THAT HAS SENT A BEAUTIFUL MESSAGE TO THE WORLD.

MUCH LOVE FROM MYSELF AND MY STAFF AT THE MAX STUDIO.

LOVE,

PETER MAX

Dear Christopher,

Dinner at that little hotel in Badminton seems a very long time ago. I wish to add to the world's chorus of admiration and respect for your staggering courage, etc. I always thought you were pretty cool. Now I think you're very cool.

> Hugh Grant
> Actor

Dear Chris—

Keep up the fight, Brother. We're all thinking of you out here.

> Love,
> Mace [William H. Macy]
> Actor

My dear Chris,

I've waited to write to you till the foam subsided; there was a time there when the reports came more intensely and frequently than commercials. I don't know what I can say in this letter that others haven't said probably more eloquently. I will mouth no homilies here, nor attempt to project what this must be like for you, for Dana, and for Matthew, Alexandra and Will.

Two things: I, who have known you in these traces perhaps longer than most, want only to tell you that the thing I loved and love most about you is not the talent, nor the celebrated shape, nor even the inestimable charm, although they have all served you splendidly to this point. It is, and always has been, the quality of your mind. The wit, perspective, clarity and joy contained in your mind is, for my money, your secret, your glory, and now your salvation. The other, of course, is to tell you how much I believe in you.

There is much to do. To achieve. To conquer. To contain. I hear you are making progress, which, no matter what you do, will not be enough, nor fast or far enough to content you. But progress is the name of the game. I look forward to more reports, and to what can synthesize from this unlooked-for twist in the wondrous rope of your life.

> Love ever,
> Jack [Jack O'Brien]
>> Artistic Director,
> Old Globe Theatre,
>> Simon Edison Centre for the
>> Performing Arts

5 JUNE '95

DAVID MAMET

DEAR CHRIS AND DANA —
WE SEND YOU ALL OUR
LOVE AND BEST WISHES —
OUR THOUGHTS ARE WITH
YOU BOTH, AND YOUR
FAMILIES.
Love DAVID

Dear Chris,

When I heard of your accident, I felt I should say something. Not just as a fellow human traveler who felt all the rage, wonder, sadness and horror at an acquaintance's new predicament, but as someone who is personally familiar with the stunning situation of having his life story suddenly transformed into something unrecognizable.

I'm not an expert on much of anything other than myself. Still, I had the urge to be encouraging. Now, after all I've heard about you, I want to send congratulations—and thanks. In the past ten years—since I was told I had an "incurable" illness that I've since been cured of; and as I was encouraged (on the best of days) to mimic only the level of success that had already been demonstrated by others—I decided that my greatest chance for satisfaction in life (whether I beat the disease or not) would be in my maniacal determination and gleeful defiance of anyone who would tell me what I could or could not accomplish. Even if I broke no new ground, I reasoned, I would at least be sending the message out to those who followed me that today's impossible is tomorrow's improbable is next Sunday's accepted norm. Unless I'm mistaken, it seems you've been astoundingly swift at pointing yourself forward and building everything that might be possible through effort and will—while continuing to explore and expand what is possible. It might just seem like getting on with your life to you. My experience tells me it's a tremendous contribution.

If there's any way I can be helpful to you—I'm available. Whether that would be through actual physical assistance, exchanging correspondence or if a lawn needs mowing. I don't know if I have much to offer, but if I'm in possession of more than I know, well . . . you and Dana are welcome to it.

> With love,
>
> Evan Handler
>
> Actor and author

SWOOSIE

Chris —
My thoughts and love and hugs are flying to you every moment.
You are *so* strong.
You are my hero.
I'm counting on you.

all my love,
Swoosie

Dear Chris,

My whole family is thinking of you and pulling for you like crazy. We know that the struggle for recovery that lies before you is gargantuan, even as we know that you will emerge victorious.

I keep referencing a proverb you hear a lot in Haiti, my adopted country, each time I think of the effort you are engaged in: "*Piti, Piti, Zwazo fe nich*"—that is, "Little by little, the bird builds its nest."

Hang in there, brother! We're with you all the way.

Love,

Jonathan [Jonathan Demme]

Director

19th October, 1995

Dear Christopher,

I am so glad to hear news of your continued recovery because you have always been someone rather special in our household. I refer particularly to the time when my son was quite young and we met you on a flight from London to America. When I told you he was a huge "Superman" fan, you were kind enough to give him a big wave when he turned around to look at you. That's the kind of thing that means a lot to soppy old parents like us, and something we won't forget in a hurry.

On behalf of the whole family I send our very best wishes to you and your family, and hope that with the help of a laugh or two from Robin Williams your recovery will be a speedy one.

Best of luck in the future and, once again, thanks for that simple gesture which meant so much.

Love,

Paul McCartney

Dearest Chris and Dana,

I think of you both often. My Pop told me he has a special place for you in his prayers each day. We went to an amazing healing ministry and this came to me for you there, Chris:

Let faith
Be
The bridge
That leaps
What is severed
In you.

May your angels keep close watch over you now.

My love always,
Stephanie Z. [Stephanie Zimbalist]
Actor

Dearest Chris—

I was shocked and heart-broken to hear of your accident, like so many others—especially the old Williamstown gang. I immediately remembered our first meeting in the basement of the church, temperature 90 degrees, humidity 150 percent. I don't know who was supposed to have played Walter Burns, but you weren't sure of this fast-talking string bean replacement actor. It turned out to be a lark, as so many of those productions were. You breathed such enthusiasm into everything—even the *Greeks*.

All of which is to say that you are thought of and prayed for daily. Extending sympathy to you is a tricky business. After all, you're not dead. I remembered the many letters we received when my father died. So many were self-serving and more concerned with acting a part than giving sympathy. When I thought of you lying there, taking stock of your situation, I thought of Roosevelt. Before his polio, he had certainly been talented, charming, effortlessly virile and intelligent. But the man that emerged from his ordeal was very different: patient, understanding, able to see very deeply into others' hearts to their secret woes, sufferings and hopes. It made him a great man.

Now, you are twice the man FDR was before his paralysis. Who knows what will emerge from your struggle? Want to run for president? We'll all vote for you! You can put some federal money back into theater! The prospects do seem restricted on one level, but so very bright on a deeper level—the level the rest of us bozos don't have time to deal with because we're so concerned with our careers. There will come a time when I will be coming to you to ask how to get through the rough patches.

It will be a hard road. If, as they say, I can do anything: send a book, write a note, visit, dance before you in my *Greeks* costume, let me know.

Bright heart of manhood, I love you.

Ever,

Ed [Edward Herrmann]

Actor

9

POLITICAL LIFE

The service we render others is the rent we pay
for our room on earth.

—Wilfred Grinfell

It is Thanksgiving 1987. The relatives have all gone home now, and Chris and I are enjoying the calm that follows a festive holiday dinner. We are chatting, cleaning up, nibbling on leftover bits of piecrust—when the phone rings.

The caller is Ariel Dorfman, the Chilean writer and activist who had defected and moved to the U.S. several years before. He is calling with a plea for help. There is a list of actors in Santiago, Chile—men and women who will be put to death within the week by members of the Pinochet regime unless some kind of effective public protest is mounted. The actors are planning to stage a rally—an illegal act itself punishable by imprisonment or death—and they want Chris to come. It will be dangerous, Dorfman says. Two days later, Chris boards a plane to Santiago.

Chris has always been willing to brave the turbulent waters of

The activist at work

politics for a cause he believes in. Equally comfortable fighting for the life of a fellow artist as for the survival of the National Endowment for the Arts, he is steadfast in his commitment and sure of his course. His ardent devotion to environmental issues on both the local and national level is legend. Like the character he once portrayed so brilliantly, he continues to fight for truth, justice and . . . well, you get the picture.

Supporting persecuted actors in Chile

Dear Christopher Reeve:

Many of us, members of the Chilean Parliament, have been deeply concerned for your health after the unfortunate accident and we have been following medical improvement through the media.

We have not forgotten the immense contribution you made a few years ago when you visited a very different Chile, in the midst of a repressive campaign against performing artists launched by the military regime. You brought the word of support, representing thousands of American actors to discourage further acts of violence against Chilean colleagues.

Your presence in those difficult and bitter days showed your commitment to human rights and decency as well as a great deal of courage. We know that you kept giving your support in every way, not only giving a monetary contribution for a documentary on Chile but were concerned in our struggle for democracy throughout the whole process. I truly believe that your bravery will help you pull through these trying times.

From the new Chile that you help and cared for so much, on behalf of the many friends you have amongst Chilean members of Parliament, I would like to express our solidarity and endless well wishes for your prompt recuperation.

> Sergio Bitar
> Senator of the Chilean Parliament

Dear Chris and family,

Deni and I are devastated by your accident and are praying for a full recovery.

Our city and country need your special intelligence, passion and civic-mindedness, which you possess in special measure.

> All our love,
> Mark [Mark Green]
> Public Advocate for the City of
> New York

Dear Chris:

Your old friends are pulling for you during these difficult days. I wish you the best.

> Sincerely,
> Paul Simon
> U.S. Senator, Illinois

Dear Christopher:

Ann and I surely have been thinking of you. We were so troubled to learn of your recent injury. I know you must feel the overwhelming love, support and good wishes of your family, friends, colleagues and fans.

I have thoroughly enjoyed my visits with you in the past regarding issues of common interest to us both, especially with regard to the worth and importance of the National Endowment for the Arts. In those visits, you always seemed to me to be a man of great courage and inner strength and I know very well that those qualities will assist you and your dear family to come through this most difficult time.

I just wanted you to know that our thoughts and our prayers go winging out to you. God bless you, Christopher. Be well.

With kindest personal regards,

most sincerely,

Al [Alan K. Simpson]

U.S. Senator, Wyoming

Dear Chris:

Your friends and colleagues in the Alliance for Clean Water Action (ACWA) join in wishing you all the best.

Working with you to protect New York State's watershed has been a pleasure and a privilege. Your appearance at our April rally in Bryant Park was tremendously successful in getting the word out on this critical issue. And, by meeting with Governor Pataki and legislative leaders in Albany, you helped us make significant progress in the fight to preserve New York's drinking water supply and its environment.

Your spirit, commitment and exuberance for life are what distinguish you as an effective activist. We're so glad those strengths can serve you now as you continue to recover.

With warmest regards,

Alan G. Hevesi,

New York City Comptroller

and members of the ACWA

THE WHITE HOUSE

WASHINGTON

September 28, 1995

Christopher Reeve
Kessler Institute for Rehabilitation
1199 Pleasant Valley Way
West Orange, New Jersey 07052

Dear Christopher:

Happy Birthday! Hillary and I hope you
had a good day. We continue to keep
you and your family in our thoughts
and prayers.

Sincerely,

Bill Clinton

*Hang in there —
A LOT of people
are praying for you.*

Chris,

You are both in my thoughts and prayers every day. Chris, I know how strong you are in mind and body—I've always admired that about you. I feel confident that you will be able to travel the road ahead with surety.

The NEA misses you. But we are so grateful for all you've given us.

Love,
Jane Alexander
Chairman, National Endowment
for the Arts

Dear Chris,

Tragedy has visited you in a terrible way. When I heard the news my heart sank and then ached for the pain you now endure. It isn't fair. It could have been avoided. A split second, a fraction of an inch, or other small variations might have spared you this. I wish I could change things, could alter the events—but I cannot.

So I will wish and pray for other things. That your breathing returns. That movement is restored. That your heart fills with the power of love, and that somehow our hopes are realized. You have helped more and more of us than you know; now it is our turn to return the favor.

Your friend always,
Bob [J. Robert Kerrey]
U.S. Senator, Nebraska

Dear Chris,

I am pleased to hear the news from your father, your mother, Ben and others in the family who have been keeping Marcelle and me posted on your progress. Each time I have called I hear more encouraging news, and you know everyone in the Leahy family is thinking of you and constantly praying for you.

Dana's words to the media have given a lot of hope to your friends and fans throughout the world, and if the good will felt towards you could heal you, you would be out of the hospital immediately.

Please tell the family they should feel free to call on me or the office at any time of day or night if there is anything we can do.

Sincerely,
Patrick [Patrick J. Leahy]
U.S. Senator, Vermont

P.S.: We are all with you, my friend.

Dear Mr. Reeve,

I'm probably the last person you would want to hear from right now, because I'm a conservative Republican from Texas. Nonetheless, I feel compelled to write because I've admired your work since I was a child.

As a physician, I can understand the anguish you must feel at this time regarding your accident. As a young father, I can appreciate the anguish you may feel for your family (and they for you) regarding the same.

Role models like you are few and far between, so keep a stiff upper lip. Our messed-up society needs "Superman" as much as he needs us.

God speed,
Tedd Mitchell, M.D.
Dallas, TX

THE WHITE HOUSE

WASHINGTON

June 14, 1996

Mr. Christopher Reeve
14 Great Hill Farms Road
Bedford, New York 10506

Dear Chris:

Thank you so much for your kind letter.
Hillary and I enjoyed speaking with you
recently, and we were thrilled to see how
well you looked.

I'm deeply grateful for your kind words
about our efforts to encourage medical research,
particularly spinal cord regeneration research.
Your inspiring optimism fills me with hope for
the many Americans with spinal cord injuries.
As always, thank you for your faith and your
leadership on this issue.

Hillary and I send our best wishes.

Sincerely,

Bill Clinton

Dear Christopher,

My husband and I were so sorry to hear the news reports of your riding accident last week. We understand you are receiving the best medical care available and no doubt the presence of your family and friends is giving you the strength to face this difficult challenge. Individuals everywhere are praying for you and we are among those who are keeping you close.

You may know that Ronnie shares your love of horses. Riding has been a part of his life for as long as I can remember and nothing could ever keep him from it. He's always felt a certain freedom when he rides—freedom to think and bathe in the silence of the outdoors. I suppose you could say that riding has been nourishment for his body and soul. No doubt you've derived similar joy from the experience over the years, and it is those sweet memories that we pray will carry you through this ordeal.

Please know that you are not alone in this, Christopher. The Lord is beside you, and your admirers are earnestly praying that you will be healed so you might one day resume the active life you were destined to live. God bless you, from both of us.

Sincerely,

Nancy Reagan

Former First Lady

Dear Mr. Christopher Reeve,

You may recall me as the person who introduced you many times to the Japanese participants of the Women's Federation for World Peace (WFWP) International Friendship Conference. In a special expression of their love, the Japanese women of the WFWP hand-made 1,000 origami cranes, which is a symbol of hope for complete recovery from illness. I would like to tell you the story of how this tradition began.

A patient who was a victim of the atomic bomb in Hiroshima had to take medicine for the radiation sickness. This medicine was wrapped in small white squares of paper. The patient had to take the medicine once a day. After she finished the medicine, she made an origami crane from each wrapper. It became her wish that each crane would represent another day of life. She began stringing the cranes into long streamers, which she hung from the ceiling, representing her wish for long life. So the doctors told her, "If you finish 1,000 rounds of this bitter medicine, you can live." It became her goal to complete 1,000 cranes.

This patient inspired a tradition in Japan. When we want to express our deepest wishes for someone's health and long life, we make 1,000 cranes. For this reason, we have made 1,000 cranes for you, to symbolize your complete recovery and long life. You are always in our prayers. May God be with you and your family.

Sincerely,

Tomiko Duggan, and all your
friends in WFWP
Washington, DC

I Knew You When . . .
(1994 to 1995)

Dear Chris,

Several summers ago in Williamstown we met briefly, as we waited to enter the auditorium at the awards ceremony for the Tennis Program at Williams College. At that time you were carrying your then infant son [Will] in his backpack. Since we were just standing there, I admired your baby, but quite frankly didn't know who you were. I just thought you were a doubly proud, gentle, tired new parent!

Your identity was not revealed to me till my son Stephen said, "Christopher Reeve's older son [Matthew] was in my group. He's a really nice kid." Stephen has been a tennis instructor there for the last two years.

Please know our thoughts and prayers are with you and your family.

Sincerely,
Lois and Jan Dorman
Slingerlands, NY

Dear Mr. Reeve,

When you were heading up to the U.S. Senate floor in the Capitol last year, I was the elevator operator who shook your hand on the way up.

After I left my elevator, I ran to my co-worker and joyously beamed about meeting someone I had wanted to meet since 1978.

In 1978, I was a 10-year-old hyperkinetic sitting in the front row of a New Jersey movie theater, watching Superman scroll before me for the fifth time. It was my first taste of a dream . . . I've since taken acting classes, and wrote and directed a play. I have you to thank for that.

I am grateful to you for your accessibility, your warmth and your handshake, given to a former goggle-eyed Senate elevator operator.

The 10-year-old in the theater is grateful for so much more.

> With deep gratitude, I am
> K.

Dear Mr. Reeve:

I was the United Airlines pilot who spoke with you briefly on your trip to Chicago last week. Now I have just heard that you have had an equestrian accident. Please be assured that my wife and I are praying for your recovery.

Hang in there!

> Very truly yours,
> Mallory McCall Horton
> Miami, FL

Dear Mr. Reeve:

No, you do not know me, but I wanted to take this opportunity to thank you for an act of kindness you performed. I do not know if you will recall the incident but last Tuesday my mother was struggling with her wheelchair on her first day at Kessler. You gave her a wide berth to pass and spoke briefly to her. I cannot tell you how much this meant. She's been flying high ever since, and more determined to work hard after seeing your accomplishments. You are setting a fine example of inner strength and perseverance.

With deepest thanks,
Marilyn Meder
Little Falls, NJ •

SOME FINAL
WORDS . . .

11 April 1996

My darling Toph,

This path we are on is unpredictable, mysterious, profoundly challenging, and, yes, even fulfilling. It is a path we chose to embark on together and for all the brambles and obstructions that have come our way of late, I have no regrets. In fact, all of our difficulties have shown me how deeply I love you and how grateful I am that we can follow this path together. Our future will be bright, my darling one, because we have each other...and our young 'uns.

With all my heart and soul I love you,

Dana

Written on the occasion of our fourth wedding anniversary,
eleven months after Chris's accident

Matthew, Dana, Chris, and Alexandra, summer 1994

Will and Chris after a hockey game, 1999

From the moment the idea for this collection of letters began forming in my head, I conceived of it as a source of raising funds for worthy causes. To that end, I have decided to donate 20 percent of my royalties from this book to the Christopher Reeve Paralysis Foundation (CRPF). By purchasing this book, you too will be contributing to those in need.

Early in 1999 the Christopher Reeve Foundation merged with the American Paralysis Association to create the Christopher Reeve Paralysis Foundation. The mission of CRPF is to raise funds for medical research leading to the effective treatment and ultimate cure for spinal-cord-injury paralysis. Additionally, through grants, CRPF supports programs that focus on aiding and improving the quality of life for all people with disabilities.

For more information about the Christopher Reeve Paralysis Foundation you may write or call:

Christopher Reeve Paralysis Foundation
500 Morris Avenue
Springfield, New Jersey 07081
(800) 225-0292

DANA REEVE is an actress, singer, mother, wife, public speaker, volunteer, and activist. She lives in New York with her husband, son, visiting stepchildren, and adopted dog, Chamois.

ABOUT THE TYPE

This book is set in Spectrum, a typeface designed
in the 1940s and the last from the distinguished
Dutch type designer Jan van Krimpen. Spectrum
is a polished and reserved font.